THE UPSTART GUIDE TO

# OWNING AND MANAGING A NEWSLETTER BUSINESS

THE UPSTART GUIDE TO
# OWNING AND MANAGING A NEWSLETTER BUSINESS

Lisa Angowski Rogak

**UPSTART PUBLISHING**
*Specializing in Small Business Publishing*
a division of Dearborn Publishing Group, Inc.

*For Margo & Squggy*

While a great deal of care has been taken to provide accurate and current information, the ideas, suggestions, general principles and conclusions presented in this text are subject to local, state, and federal laws and regulations, court cases, and any revisions of same. Neither the author nor the publisher of this book is engaged in rendering, by the sale of this book, legal, accounting, or other professional services. The reader is thus urged to employ the services of a competent professional in such matters.

Executive Editor: Bobbye Middendorf
Managing Editor: Jack Kiburz
Cover Design: Paul Perlow Design

Published by Upstart Publishing Company, Inc.,
a division of Dearborn Publishing Group, Inc.

Printed in the United States of America

95  96  97   10  9  8  7  6  5  4  3  2  1

**Library of Congress Cataloging-in-Publication Data**
Rogak, Lisa Angowski.
     The upstart guide to owning and managing a newsletter business / by
Lisa Angowski Rogak.
        p.   cm.
     Includes index.
     ISBN 0-936894-87-3
     1. Newsletters     I. Title.
PN4784.N5R64   1995                                    95-6806
070.1'75—dc20                                          CIP

# CONTENTS

# PREFACE

Whenever I tell people that I publish and edit news-letters, odds are that they'll say the following: Oh, you must have been good at English in school."

Invariably, they're a bit surprised when I tell them that I hated English in school, and loved algebra instead, because I thought it was just like doing crossword puzzles, which I could do all day.

Sometimes, this exchange might follow: Oh, then you must have loved geometry, right?"

*Wrong.* Whenever I was confronted with trying to prove why angle A equaled angle B, but could have never equaled angle C, I always felt like pointing to the triangle in question and saying, "Because it *looks* like it does."

Publishing a newsletter is a little bit like my version of geometry, combined with a little bit of algebra. You pick a topic because it looks like it will fly, and then everything else that's involved in your newsletter's launch is done pretty much on instinct with a good bit of puzzle-solving thrown in, from deciding how many copies of your first issue to print, to how you're going to market it and attract subscribers.

I didn't like English in high school because the class was asked to mimic a certain style that the teacher was looking for. And I didn't like geometry because it involved too much logic. I should have realized even back then that I would always fail miserably whenever I worked at a job for someone else: "What do you mean I have to be here at the same time for the same amount of time every day?"

Publishing a newsletter will appeal to anyone who believes passionately enough in a particular topic to want to invest their time and money in it. It's also important that you feel strongly about letting other people know how you feel about your subject. Sometimes, in fact, your interest may run close to that of an obsession. Unlike high school English, you won't have to conform to writing in a style just so someone else will like it. Except for a writing style where you try to pack as much useful information into each issue as you can, it's possible to be as opinionated as you want in your newsletter, and your readers will love you for it.

Even if you've written or edited another publication for someone else, you should be prepared for a surprise when you start to publish your own newsletter. Not only will you be writing and editing detailed articles on a single subject and exploring your topic in-depth over a number of years, but you will also find out what it's like to run your own show, which as anyone can tell you will be quite different from working for somebody else. After all, the buck will stop with you and only you—every time.

Even though publishing a newsletter involves a lot of hard work, the rewards are ample: instant expert status, in-depth knowledge on a particular topic, and what is effectively your own forum in each and every issue, not to mention the eventual financial rewards that come with your persistence.

Once you start publishing your own newsletter, I'll warn you now that the skills you'll need and the headiness of having your own publication will get into your blood. Even if you go on to write or edit professionally for other publishers—which may be one of the reasons why you want to publish a newsletter in the first place—the experience of doing it all will always stay with you. So consider yourself forewarned.

Oh, and one more thing. Even if you did love English and geometry in school, you're still fully capable of publishing a newsletter. As you learn about the intricacies of running a business, you'll find that the instinctual side of your personality will start to poke its head out in order to combine with the logical side of you and result in a great newsletter.

# OPPORTUNITIES AS A NEWSLETTER PUBLISHER

I f you want to start publishing a newsletter on a certain topic to sell on a subscription basis, the good news is that it's both cheap—if you want it to be—and easy to start. However, once you start publishing your own newsletter, you may find that you will frequently encounter one or all of the following reactions:

- Is that all there is?
- Do you really expect me to pay that much money for a subscription?
- Why don't you just publish a magazine instead of pretending that you want to be one?

Then there's the flip side of the newsletter business. Since, by its very merits, a newsletter is supposed to deliver concise, timely information about a specific niche within a particular subject, those people who are interested in that subject frequently react in a different way. Some of the instances I've heard of are:

- they tear open the envelope the minute they retrieve it from the mailbox, sit down on the floor, and read it right then and there, cover to cover;
- they hoard every copy and keep them in a fireproof box;
- they write to the publisher and ask what they need to do to become a lifetime subscriber.

Today, it's estimated that anywhere from 100,000 to 200,000 different newsletters are published each year. Even I was shocked when I read these figures, but when you start to think about the wide variety of newsletters that you probably already receive—from the PTA, your church, your dentist, and maybe even that famous penny-pinching newsletter or another that contains nothing but chocolate recipes, as well as the one your company publishes for its employees and stockholders four times a year—well, then, this figure begins to make sense.

If you want to publish your own newsletter, you should know that you probably already possess all the skills that you'll need to do so. You'll just need to do your homework first.

## What Exactly Is a Newsletter, Anyway?

Typically, a newsletter is a publication that is published about a specific subject or for a particular group. As such, the publication may go into great detail on the subject, details that may bore the casual observer but would thrill a person who's seriously interested in the topic.

A newsletter can be as brief as one page or as long as 32— and I've seen newsletters that are even longer. A newsletter may be published once a year or once a day, may be created with a typewriter or the latest in desktop publishing software, and may be run off with an old-fashioned mimeograph machine or on fancy textured paper with several colors of ink and color photos. And you could have 20 readers or 200,000. In the following chapters, I'll help you explore which of these types are best for your publication; most newsletters fall in the middle of this spectrum, with the exception of circulation, where many newsletter publishers are ecstatic if they can claim 1,000 subscribers.

A newsletter can also be a perfect way to impart information to members of an association who rely on it as a way to find out about upcoming events and news about the group. However, this is a different type of newsletter, since it's not sold by subscription. A business may also decide to develop a promotional newsletter to keep customers as well as attract new ones, whereas a church group or trade organization may use a newsletter to keep its members informed about news that concerns the group. Since both these types tend to be free, this is not the type of newsletter I'm going to be exploring in this book. Instead, I will tell you how to publish a newsletter to sell by subscription only.

Some people may think that you want to publish a newsletter because you can't afford to publish a magazine—or are too lazy. The truth is that the subjects of most newsletters are far too specific to warrant the expense and volume of a magazine, which is supported more by its advertisers than by the subscription fees of its readers. In addition, the majority of newsletters don't accept advertising.

But a newsletter offers several advantages over a magazine, which is why there are at least ten times more newsletters out there—at least—than magazines. Here are just a few:

- Since you're not supported by advertising, you don't have to worry about offending an advertiser by something you may say in the newsletter.

- Newsletter production is pretty straightforward, so the amount of time you'll spend on writing, designing, and printing your publication is much less involved than a magazine. This way, you can add late-breaking news up to an hour before you bring it to the printer or copy shop.

- The more specific you get in your newsletter articles, the more your readers will love it, which means you'll get to explore all the topics you may have felt would have been too insignificant for a larger audience. For instance, in a newsletter about model trains, an article about one of the early designers would be welcomed. In a more general magazine about hobbies, it would probably be too specific.

- A newsletter also means there's a good chance you'll be able to handle all of the work yourself—at least in the beginning. You may even be able to do it on a part-time basis. Besides, when you first start publishing your newsletter, you probably won't be able to afford to hire any employees, anyway. By the time you're ready, you'll know your market, your topic, and your business inside and out. You will be able to impart this information to an employee much more readily than in the beginning. (See Chapter 6 for more information about hiring employees.)

You can publish a newsletter out of your home or by "borrowing" your computer after hours at your regular job. And even if you have the writing down pat but feel intimidated by the idea of designing and laying out a newsletter, with the explosion in desktop publishing, you'll find that your next-door neighbor will be glad to help you out—or even take on the job. Today's desktop software programs make it easy to design and layout a professional-looking newsletter in an afternoon, even if you have no eye for what looks good on the printed page at all.

Also, a newsletter is a great way to get your voice out in the world, even if it's just to a small audience. Whether your writing has been published before or not, the idea of putting your thoughts and ideas out there for others to read can be heady stuff indeed. And when you hear how something you wrote has changed someone's life—believe me, it happens, even with the smallest newsletter—well, that's enough to keep you going when things get rough.

## A Day in the Life of a Newsletter

I'll tell you right now, the best thing about publishing a newsletter is that every day is different.

What's the worst?

Why, the fact that every day is different. How you handle this simple fact depends on the type of person you are. If you thrive on order and predictability, you may not be comfortable running a newsletter business—or any business at all, for that matter. Especially in the beginning stages of starting your newsletter when you're probably doing everything yourself, you'll find yourself handling everything from conducting an interview with one of the leading experts in your field to licking envelopes and stuffing them with a copy of your brochure or direct mail letter. You may also receive a call from your printer to let you know that he or she ran out of the paper stock that you like and won't have more until next Wednesday. Then, as soon as you hang up with the printer, you may hear from a subscriber who loved your last issue and wants to renew his or her subscription for another year.

Currently, I'm publishing two newsletters: *Travel Marketing Bulletiin,* a marketing newsletter for small travel businesses, which comes out nine times a year, and *Sticks,* for people who want to move to the country, which I publish bimonthly, or six times a year. What follows is a fairly typical day, which again means that it is anything *but:*

**8 A.M.:** The phone rings on my 800 line. It's a man on the west coast who's up early and wants to subscribe to *Sticks* with his MasterCard. I write down the information and fill out an order form, a credit card slip, address an envelope, and put the current issue inside, and add his name and address to my computerized database and subscription list. This scenario will be repeated at least five more times that day with this newsletter, and three times for *Travel Marketing Bulletin*. I'll also receive calls from an average of 15 people who call for information on each newsletter. For them, I'll again address an envelope, put a brochure in it, place a stamp on the envelope, and add their name to the prospect file on my computer.

**8:30 A.M.:** I'll review my list of what needs to be done that day, which includes a mailing to 50 radio show producers, phoning a couple of my freelance writers to talk about article ideas for the upcoming issues, calling the printer to order 500 more copies of my new brochure, and researching a couple of stories for one of the newsletters. Of course, with the way the phone rings and with the onslaught of mail I deal with every day, I'll be lucky if I'm able to cross off half of the items on my list. I start printing out the cover letters for the media mailing on my laser printer.

**9:20 A.M.:** The phone rings. It's an account executive from a New York public relations firm wanting to know if I'll run a story on her client in *Travel Marketing Bulletin*. I tell her that it doesn't seem likely, given the fact that neither she nor her client has ever seen a copy of the newsletter.

**9:45 A.M.:** A writer sends her article—three days late—over the fax. Since I usually have writers send their stories in on disk to save typing time on my end, not to mention my wrists, I stop what I'm doing and start typing the story directly into the newsletter layout. As soon as I'm finished, I can send the completed camera-ready newsletter through my modem to my printer. In the past, I've had to drive it there myself.

**10:05 A.M.:** A man in Milwaukee calls to get a sample copy of *Sticks* after he read about it in his local paper.

**10:20 A.M.:** A subscriber calls to order a copy of a new book on marketing I've just begun to sell through *Travel Marketing Bulletin*. Since I don't like to keep money or storage space tied up in inventory, I order from the publisher as soon as I get a request. When I finish taking the order, I call my sales rep at the publisher, who sends me out a copy the same day, along with a bill.

**10:30 A.M.:** I go back to typing the story into the newsletter.

**10:32 A.M.:** The phone rings. It's a radio producer who wants to set up a live phone interview with me the day after tomorrow. I prepare a mailing label and call an express mail company to pick up the package, since the producer and the host need to review the material before the show.

**10:45 A.M.:** I return to the computer.

**11:15 A.M.:** I finish typing in the story and do some light editing on it. I press a couple of buttons and a few seconds later it's in my print shop's computer. A few days later I will send my updated mailing list the same way—the printer also stuffs the envelopes and sends the newsletter out—so that people who have become new subscribers since the last issue will be added to the printer's master list.

**11:25 A.M.:** I go back to printing out letters for the press mailing. I finish the letters and start sifting through the mail, which has just arrived.

**11:43 A.M.:** It seems that one of the subscription checks I deposited last week bounced. I subtract the amount from my checking account, remove the name from the subscription list, and call up the computer file that contains the letter I regularly send to deadbeats like this one. After I tack on a $20 handling fee—what my bank charges me plus five bucks to me for the hassle—I usually don't hear from the subscriber again. Either they're too embarrassed or they think it's too expensive. Most often, I end up writing the bank fee off as a tax deductible business expense. I don't mind this as much as the fact that it's interrupted the flow of my day.

**12:15 P.M.:** I turn the answering machine on and leave the office for an hour. Without this break each day, I'll be cranky and tired by 3:00.

**1:30 P.M.:** Back in the office with five messages on the answering machine, all from people who want more information about the newsletters. They always seem to call during lunch time!

**1:55 P.M.:** 50 press kits to stuff and get out by 4:00, and I've only finished the cover letters. I still have to staple press releases, select which sample copies and press clips I'm going to send, put it all in the folder, stuff and stamp the envelope, and put the address labels on the envelopes, all in the next two hours. It may not sound like much, but this is why answering machines were invented. I resolve to ignore the phone—or at least screen the messages—so I can finish this job which is already a few days late.

**3:55 P.M.:** I make it to the post office as the mail pickup truck pulls in ahead of me. My mailing makes it out today with minutes to spare.

**4:10 P.M.:** Back in the office. Four people have called since I've been gone. It's not just that people wait until lunch to call, I think; they wait until they sense I'm out of the office. Some days I love the phone while on others, I hate it. I proceed to return all the calls.

**4:40 P.M.:** I discover I didn't call any of the people on my list today. That means it goes to the top of the list for tomorrow. I make another To Do list.

**4:50 P.M.:** The phone rings. It's a subscriber who wants to write an article for the next issue.

**5:10 P.M.:** We hang up, with me encouraging the subscriber to restrict the topic, making it more narrow. While I've been on the phone, two more calls have come in and were forwarded to my fax line, which also has an answering machine hooked up to take messages. I return the calls.

**5:30 P.M.:** I start to close up the office for the day, but like always, I realize that I could easily spend another ten hours here and not get everything done that I need to do. This is one reason why I do most of my writing in the evening or on the weekends, when the phone doesn't ring as much and my concentration is better.

## Running the Numbers

As I've already mentioned, the number of newsletters that are published today is staggering. Though the majority of them may be free publications distributed to members of an organization, there are many newsletters that are run as stand-alone businesses, as mine are.

Although newsletters have been around since the 18th century, the newsletter as a form of communication seems to have proliferated in great numbers only since the 1970s. There are several reasons why:

- While the generations of the 1950s and 60s were a mainstream generation where everyone listened to the same music, read the same magazines and books, and watched the same TV shows, today's generations are highly fragmented and growing even more splintered each day. Newsletters benefit from this fragmentation because of their very nature: to appeal to a small, well-defined niche market.

- People are demanding more information in all fields than they used to. They expect a resource to be there on an obscure topic when they go looking for it. Undoubtedly, as people became more and more interested in the kind of information that gets more specific each year, the nature of newsletter topics will also become more specific.

Newsletters are also beginning to explore the vast corners of the Internet. There are already many bulletin boards on the computer networks that could be considered to be similar to newsletters in content, format, and the rabid attention of its readers. Only time will tell how far you will be able to go with electronic publishing.

## Your Primary Product

If you are publishing a newsletter, the publication will be your primary product. It's likely, however, that eventually you will be involved in producing other related products that are connected with the newsletter. (See Ancillary Products and Services for more information on additional products you can sell that will increase your revenue.)

When you publish a newsletter, you are offering nothing but pure information to your customers. Of course, that information will be tinged with your opinion, but it is still only information.

But that's OK, because that's why your subscribers have chosen your newsletter. In reality, they could gather all that information themselves, but it would take up a lot of time, which they don't have. So they look to your newsletter as a digest of sorts, a way to gather information that's important to them without having to dig through tons of journals, papers, or books to get it.

Through your newsletter, you are also selling your expertise and your opinion: You publish what you think your readers need to know about. It's as simple as that. But just because you're selling information in the form of a newsletter doesn't necessarily mean that you have to limit your forum to just a newsletter.

## Ancillary Products and Services

This is where the extras come in. A favorite saying among newsletter publishers is: "The newsletter is my bread and butter. My other products are where I really make my money."

The other products, are everything from books on your specific topic—whether you publish them or somebody else does—Special Reports, which are nothing more than long articles, seminars, private consultations, or even premium products, like coffee mugs or a calendar with the newsletter name stamped on it to serve as a constant reminder. When you're offering these products for sale to your subscribers, in essence, you're preaching to the converted. You'll find that the revenue from ancillary products will not only add significantly to your bottom line, but your profit margin will also be higher. For example, with a newsletter, you need to incur a certain amount of expense with every issue that you produce and send out. Printing, postage, and writer's fees, to name a few. With an ancillary product like a mug or a sweatshirt, you produce it once and that's it. And if you buy these ancillary products in volume, your costs go down and your profits go up.

Sometimes, you may find that you're able to spin off yet another newsletter from your existing newsletter and create yet another niche within a niche. For instance, from *Sticks* I'm thinking of spinning off a new monthly publication called, *Jobs & Business Opportunities in the Sticks,* a newsletter that is nothing but help wanted ads and businesses that are available for sale or rent in rural areas all over the country. Right now, it's a special insert in the newsletter. Why would I create it? Because my readers kept on telling me that the number one reason why they didn't move to the country was that they couldn't—or didn't know how to—find a decent job. I added to their knowledge and to my circulation and revenues by creating another useful piece of information for my readers. I'm still mulling over whether to spin it off as a separate publication.

Over time, once you get your newsletter off the ground, you'll find that your own subscribers and potential subscribers will ask you about items and services that you probably didn't even know existed. And after doing a bit of research, if you discover that the product or service doesn't exist, perhaps you'll decide to go ahead and start it yourself. After all, you do have a captive audience who is eager for more information on your given subject. Why not give it to them?

## Finding Your Niche

Most readers will decide to subscribe to your newsletter based on one question alone:

> "Will it help me to improve my life in some way?"

That's it. And if through your promotional material (see Chapter 7 for more information about marketing your newsletter) they feel that you won't be able to help them answer this question in the affirmative, then they won't subscribe. It's as simple as that.

The topic that you choose for your newsletter should be as well-defined as possible, yet it shouldn't be so narrow so that no one will have a use for it. But you'll also want your audience to be sizable.

Contrary to what this may mean, it's not too difficult to select a topic, narrow it down, and still be sure that your universe of subscribers is still substantial. Here are the common categories of newsletters that are out there:

***Business.*** Slanted towards a particular area of business, a business newsletter focuses on providing both late-breaking news in the industry as well as giving lots of ideas for how to do your job or run your business better. There's *communications briefings* to help people to communicate better in their jobs, and *Boardroom Reports,* a popular newsletter that digests information mostly about work and careers.

*Consumer.* A consumer-oriented newsletter helps people improve their personal lives. Some examples are the many health newsletters out there, like *The Mayo Clinic Health Letter* and *Medical Abstracts.* There's also *The Tightwad Gazette.*

*Special Interest.* These types of newsletters are usually for people who are interested in a particular hobby. Most often, they are included as part of a membership in an organization that specializes in that topic. As such, a newsletter publisher would rarely decide to publish a newsletter like this, except as a labor of love.

*Association.* These newsletters provide members of a social, non-profit group with news about the association, sometimes along with a calendar. Again, serious subscription newsletter publishers tend to leave these to the groups that already publish them. Even if there was some money to be made from publishing such a newsletter and getting members to subscribe, some potential subscribers would probably resent the fact that an outsider is producing the newsletter. Indeed, most association newsletters are produced entirely by volunteers.

## Refining Your Newsletter Idea

You already have a topic in mind for your newsletter. What you need to do now is refine your idea, check to see if any other newsletter is already being published—though it doesn't necessarily matter if you have competition—and put your own unique spin on the topic.

Say you want to produce a newsletter that addresses the problems of working mothers. Great. But there's already a magazine out on the topic—*Working Mother*—that hundreds of thousands of women read each month. How will yours be different?

Well, you think you want to focus on time management techniques for working mothers. OK. The first thing you should do is to find out how many articles you can think of for this topic. And remember, each article should tell the reader how she can improve some facet of her life.

A good rule of thumb is to come up with 100 ideas in order to decide that you're going to make your newsletter fly. Are you stuck at 17? If they don't come pouring out of you, you might want to rethink your topic. I think the topic of time management for working mothers is too broad, and it also isn't sexy enough, which is a necessary component for consumer newsletters if you plan to promote your newsletter through publicity. In fact, what kind of information could you provide for the executive woman that the mother who works as a secretary could benefit from too? I don't think it would work in a newsletter. Here's a hint that will help narrow your niche: In this case, since the executive mother is used to reading a lot of books, magazines, and newsletters to improve both her work and parenting skills—and knows that she'll have to pay money to receive good, specific advice—narrowing your newsletter toward women who hold white-collar mid-management and higher jobs would be a good bet.

But for her, again, the issue of managing her time better may just be too broad of a topic. Besides, she probably learns a lot about how to manage her time from all the professional literature she reads. Is there a certain area where she could use specific advice on managing her time at home and with her family?

Here's another hint: Where do working mothers tend to cut corners most in order to spend more time with their families? In the kitchen, resulting in more meals eaten out and a greater tendency toward meals that are high in fat and calories, which is not the healthiest diet.

So how about a newsletter for working mothers showing them how to prepare nutritious meals for their families in less time? The consumer won't be interested in articles that provide cooking tips. Instead, how about a newsletter with nothing but menus and recipes and shopping lists for the whole week. Describe how the meals can provide leftovers for lunch and microwave meals, but only take a few hours of her time on the weekend to throw together, and is healthy to boot? Although this is not a new idea—I've seen it done in women's magazines—I think a newsletter providing a month's worth of menu planning geared toward the seasons and variations would be a big hit. Taking different ages and food preferences into account would also be helpful. You should feel free to go ahead and use this idea—I have no time to do another newsletter, even though I have ideas for at least ten more.

My point in taking you through this step-by-step process is to make sure that your newsletter is helpful enough and the market is sizable enough, while providing the reader with information in a usable format. And it would be easy to promote.

By the way, if you discover that a newsletter on your carefully targeted subject already exists, twist it some more—either slant it towards another group or format it in an entirely different way.

## How Your Lifestyle Will Change

Go back and reread the earlier section, "Typical Business Day." Unless you've already run your own business, life as you know it now will cease to exist once you start publishing a newsletter on a regular schedule. One comment that I hear from newsletter publishers of all types is that most tasks always take twice as long as they think they will, from writing an article to laying out an issue to waiting for the responses to your direct mail offer to start rolling in. And if you're an impatient person to begin with—like me—these delays will occasionally make you crazy and unhappy with your business. And in the beginning, everything takes longer than you think, whether it's fine-tuning the layout and design of your newsletter or setting up your new phone system.

My advice is to dig in your heels for the long run, because your lifestyle will also change for the better. The first surprise is that people will view you as an expert in your subject even though you may have just been dabbling in the topic as a hobby up until now. This may mean that the media will call you for quotes, subscribers will look at you reverently at conferences and trade shows, and you may be asked by another publisher to write a book on the topic.

Most newsletter publishers start out by running their business out of their homes and on a part-time basis. Consider this a warning: If you've never worked at home or for yourself before, be prepared for a big surprise. The business will do its best to spill over into every corner of your life—that is, if you let it. That's why it's a good idea to take a break at least once a week, even if your natural inclination is to work around the clock.

You may be all gung-ho about starting to publish a newsletter, but you should take some time to consider the other members of your family and how they might feel. You should be sure that your spouse and family are in total agreement with your plans. While you may be doing most of the work, the fact is that they may be asked to pitch in every so often to help with stuffing envelopes, proofreading copy, and tolerating your absence both physically and mentally. Make sure they understand you're running the business for the benefit of the entire family. Even if one person in your household is opposed to the idea, you should work out your differences before you begin to publish your newsletter. Play it safe. Before you proceed with your plans, be sure that you sit down with all family members to get their feedback.

## Income and Profit Potentials

As is the case with any new business, in the beginning it may seem as though you're working for free. You may end up pouring every penny of revenue back into the newsletter, perhaps for a new computer system, more ads or brochures, or renting a booth at a trade show.

Don't worry. A newsletter doesn't require that you invest a huge amount of cash or that you tie up a significant amount of money from the beginning in overhead or inventory like other businesses. If you work hard at keeping your expenses down while increasing your subscription lists with inexpensive marketing techniques (see Chapter 7), in time you'll be able to farm more work out and pay yourself a salary as well.

The amount of money you'll be able to eventually realize from your newsletter depends on how much marketing you'll do as well as the universe of potential subscribers. In addition, your subscription rate and overall success at developing and selling ancillary products will play a key role in your success.

Of course, hiring an employee or subcontracting some of the work out to other businesses will eat into your expenses. But at the same time, it will free up some of your time so that you can concentrate your energy on tasks to bring in more subscribers and more revenue. If you can, leave the simpler tasks to someone else, whether it's a mailing house or an employee.

Once your newsletter is established and your renewal rate is above 50 percent (we'll discuss this vital aspect of newsletter publishing in Chapter 7), you may be astounded at the profits you'll pull in. For instance, if you publish a monthly newsletter for $48 and have 1,000 subscribers, your gross—without ancillary products—will be $48,000. The costs of producing your newsletter—printing, postage, research costs, phone bills, etc.—may run to half of that, if that high. Therefore, your profit is 50 percent. The more subscribers you have, the more profit you'll make.

## Risk Potential

Anyone who starts any business will face a certain amount of risk. Though statistics say that 90 percent of new magazines won't make it to see their fifth anniversaries, the survival rate for newsletters is much healthier.

For one, production costs are lower so you don't have to scramble to pay huge printing and postage bills for each issue that you send out. And you need to attract a smaller number of subscribers in order to continue publishing. Most newsletters will make it on 1,000 new subscriptions each year—and some of the higher priced newsletters rely on only a fraction of that.

Your chances for making it to your fifth anniversary are much improved if your topic is suitably narrow, you've determined that your audience is large enough, and if you provide usable information that is not readily available elsewhere. Injecting a healthy dose of your own opinion into the editorial also helps, and in fact is unavoidable when you decide the topic and slant of your articles for the newsletter. On this last point, however, you shouldn't go overboard.

Case in point: When I started to publish one of my newsletters, I discovered that there were already two others published on the same subject. This caused me to pause for a moment, but not enough to quit entirely. I sent for sample copies.

After reviewing them, I was able to breathe a sigh of relief. One was nothing more than statistics about the topic written without much of the editor's opinion apparent and in a breezy style—which is anathema to the traditional no-nonsense, tightly-written newsletter style. It was also priced way too high. The editorial in the other newsletter contained too much

19

opinion, as the copy consisted mostly of the editor ranting and raving about his perceived competition—which would soon include me—and berating his readers for not spending more money on the services that he offered. His layout was also done in an amateur, haphazard fashion. Both publishers, I later learned, complained about their low renewal rates.

Well, no wonder. If you don't provide any useful information that readers can use, they're not going to renew, and they might just cancel their subscriptions in the middle and ask for a refund on undelivered issues.Look through one of the newsletter directories to find your competition.(See Chapter 3 for a listing of the directories. Some may be found at your local library.) Then study their publications and define your own newsletter in a different way to increase your chances of success in the field. The good news is that if you find several newsletters on the same subject, the audience is probably large enough to support one more. *Yours.*

## Action Guidelines

✔ Realize that publishing your newsletter will be a bona fide business, where you'll probably work harder than ever before.

✔ Consider what type of niche you'd like your newsletter to fill, as well as the audience you'd like to reach.

✔ Talk candidly with your family about how starting a newsletter business will change all of your lives.

✔ Expect some risk; publishing can be a highly volatile business.

✔ Be prepared to be treated as an expert in your field.

## Newsletter Publisher Profile

### Lisa Angowski Rogak
*Sticks*
*Travel Marketing Bulletin*

I stumbled into newsletter publishing before I even knew what I was doing. In fact, it was only after I had launched my fourth and fifth newsletter titles that I was able to realize the breadth, hard work, and rewards that publishing a newsletter entailed.

I first learned about newsletters when I was working part-time for a public relations firm in New York. One of the company's accounts was a newsletter, and I would occasionally write press releases and make media phone calls on behalf of the newsletter in between helping out on the agency's other accounts, which included both doctors and financial planners.

I spent the rest of my time away from the job trying to make it as a freelance magazine writer. All the books on writing that I had read had always directed beginning writers to "write about what you know." At the time, what I knew about were the eating disorders anorexia nervosa and bulimia. Although I had written both personal experience stories and factual articles on the topics, I couldn't find any magazines that wanted to publish them.

One afternoon, I was sitting at my kitchen table looking at all of my rejected articles. The newsletter at work had popped into my mind, and voila, I thought about turning all of my rejected articles into a newsletter. Then I would write a press release and send them out to magazines and newspapers that might write about my newsletter.

These were the days before desktop computers were everywhere, so I brought my articles to a typesetter and instructed him to assemble them in a newsletter format. I also had stationery printed up and within a week, I was on my way.

Eating disorders as a newsworthy topic was just beginning to catch on back then in 1982, so with my newsletter—which was titled *Consuming Passions*—I was among the first to ride the crest of the wave. Because I was first, magazines as diverse as *Ms., Woman's Day,* and *Seventeen* wrote small articles about the newsletter, always giving information on subscription costs as well as my address. I was also interviewed on many radio and TV shows about the topic. When Karen Carpenter died from the effects of anorexia nervosa in 1983, I was the first person many media people called for a quote. It was then I realized that publishing a newsletter had rendered me an expert on the subject. Indeed, many of the newsletter publishers I speak to today tell me that they sometimes look over their shoulder when someone addresses them as an expert in their field. I'll admit, publishing a newsletter is the quickest way to become an expert in a certain field—that is, if you aren't one already.

I had started writing about eating disorders as a form of therapy and also as a way to launch my freelance writing career. As an editor of a regular publication, other editors— some of whom were the same ones who had rejected the articles I put into my first issue of *Consuming Passions*—began to give me magazine assignments. I wrote about the subject of eating disorders, yes, but also on other health topics, and eventually I turned to travel writing. After two years of publishing *Consuming Passions,* I began to tire of the subject. It had also ceased to be a personal problem for me, so I sold the newsletter.

I spent the next few years writing for magazines, but publishing a newsletter had remained in my blood, and I began to look around for a way to publish another. I had been lifting weights for several years at that point, and I read the muscle magazines regularly. I had noticed that these magazines were pretty much the same from one issue to the next, and that they didn't pay much attention to women who were working out with weights. There was also a huge controversy in the field about contests being fixed and weighted toward those men and women who were particularly photogenic, which outraged me and many others.

So I began publishing my second newsletter, *The Bodybuilding Woman,* which contained some training information, some contest reporting, and a whole lot of railing against the ingrained system. I sent sample copies and press releases to the muscle magazines, all of whom wrote something about the newsletter over the two years I was publishing it. I also started another newsletter at this point called *SporTreks,* for people who were interested in finding out about active travel opportunities. I stopped publishing *The Bodybuilding Woman* after a couple of years because I had moved 30 miles from the nearest gym and began to lose interest in the sport. Also, my constant railing had garnered me a lot of supporters, but hadn't changed anything within the sport, which was one of my naive goals from the beginning. *SporTreks* never really took off—the travel and outdoor magazines were much more able to accurately convey what it was like to go on certain trips than an eight-page newsletter could. And so, with no newsletters to publish, I went back to freelance writing.

This time, I started writing books for other publishers instead of magazine articles. But again, I still wanted to publish another newsletter, partly because I could control my words instead of being edited by someone else, and I felt I could control my fate better than if I continued to write for other publishers.

And so I started *Sticks,* a bimonthly newsletter for people in the city and suburbs who want to move to the country. At the time I conceived of the idea for the newsletter, I was actually living in Boston and thoroughly miserable. I lasted two months in the city before I moved back to the boonies. It was easy for me to move, and I knew what to expect since I had lived there before, but what about other people who may have wanted to move to the country, but couldn't?

After planning the first issue, writing the press kit and saving up some money for the initial printing and postage, I launched *Sticks* in March of 1994. The response from my initial media mailing was immediate—*US News & World Report* called three days after I had mailed out the kit. They quoted me in an article about small-town living and gave the subscription information for my newsletter. And with an early prestigious clip like that, I was able to parlay it into getting other major appearances in *New York Magazine, Country Living, Snow Country, House Beautiful,* and many other publications in the first six months. Today, I maintain the steady stream of orders with more publicity, some advertising, and generally improving the content of the newsletter.

As I was launching *Sticks,* I knew I would be repeating the process in a couple of months with another newsletter that also grew out of my personal experience. When I was spending my time working as a travel writer, writing books, and articles, I frequently stayed in small inns and B&Bs. I customarily spent a lot of time with the innkeeper, talking about everything from getting into the business to marketing the inn.

Whenever I mentioned this last topic, most innkeepers and B&B hosts wrinkled their noses. They should be doing more, they told me, but after all, they didn't have marketing backgrounds and they didn't know quite what to do beyond advertising and updating their brochure every year.

Well, I've always loved to market, and that's what I spent most of my time doing as a freelance writer, trying to get more assignments. So I would give the innkeepers ideas about the different things they could try to improve their marketing. More than one of them told me that I should write a book about marketing for innkeepers.

How about a newsletter instead? So that's what I did, and published the first issue in May, 1994. I will eventually publish a book on the topic.

I'm going to launch another newsletter in 1995—see the Appendices for my Business and Marketing Plan—and I have ideas for at least several other consumer and trade newsletters kicking around. The difference now is that I've learned not to do everything myself. I farm out writing work and telephone work, and I have employees to help me with the day-to-day marketing, which is what consumes the most time in the whole operation. Before, I could handle two newsletters by myself. Now, with all the ancillary products and other future publishing projects, I've realized that I can't do it all myself, even though it seems that I work harder now with employees than before. One spinoff from *Travel Marketing Bulletin* is a directory of inns and B&Bs for business travelers to be produced on computer disk and marketed in-house in the spring of 1995.

Publishing newsletters has made it possible for me to feel secure about publishing my own work and the work of others, as well as confident enough to proceed to the next level, a field I've been hesitant about entering for some time: publishing books. Whether the books I publish will be tied into the newsletters or freestanding titles, I'll be the first to admit that it was publishing newsletters that allowed me to get to this point.

Chapter

2

# REQUIREMENTS

B efore you proceed to run headfirst into writing articles
and planning future issues of your newsletter, it's a
good idea to take some time to evaluate yourself, your
financial situation, and the skills you'll need to publish your
newsletter. Doing your homework at this stage will save you
from making big and possibly costly mistakes down the road.

## Assessing Your Personal Goals

First, you must determine what your overall personal goals are
and how publishing a newsletter fits in with them—and vice
versa.

Take some time to answer the following questions in detail:
- What are the three main reasons why you want to publish a newsletter?
- Why do you think you want to run a business that
  involves tight and endless deadlines and work that is frequently isolating?

- How long to you plan to publish the newsletter?
- Do you view publishing your newsletter as a part- or a full-time business?
- What are your personal goals aside from publishing your newsletter? Do you plan to retire at a certain age, or move on to something else after running the business for ten years?

As you've already surmised, the fantasy of publishing a newsletter does not even begin to match the reality—even though you won't fully admit to this until you're knee-deep in the business. Many newsletter publishers view the business as a means to an end: It provides a way they can go into semi- or early retirement, or the only way they can finally move to the country and be able to make a living. Or else they can publish a newsletter on the topic they've been consulting others about—either informally or professionally for years.

Other people dream of the self-sufficiency they'll be able to achieve by running their own business. Certainly some people who want to give up long commutes to an unsatisfying job or spend more time with their families will begin to publish a newsletter for this reason.

Publishing a newsletter is like any other business: You need it to provide income along with a healthy dose of satisfaction. You also need to have something in your life besides the business. That's why it's important to set goals for yourself that are totally separate from the business. Burnout is very common when you publish a newsletter, where you'll face constant deadlines, and one way to prevent it is to plan your personal goals—that is, those that have absolutely nothing to do with the business—in advance. Whether your goal is to learn a foreign language, or spend more time with your friends and family, in this business, it is both possible and very necessary.

## Assessing Your Personal Values

If you're looking to publish your own newsletter because you want it to serve as a forum for your own personal views, forget it unless you have a nationally syndicated radio show, like to make inflammatory comments that appeal to a good number of Americans, and your initials are R.L. Come to think of it, he already has a newsletter. So unless you have a strong following that hangs on your every word—this applies to many best-selling authors of nonfiction—forget about starting to develop your reputation in a newsletter unless you have a subject to base it on. It would be a bit like a vanity press. Better to have others—book publishers and TV talk show hosts—extol your virtues so you can build a mailing list and then publish your own newsletter.

It may provide no useful information to readers, except as a vehicle for you.

The kind of person who would excel at publishing a newsletter has the following traits:

- Knows a lot about a particular subject, but always wants to know more.

- Has a reasonable grasp of the different ways to deliver information to readers: feature articles, columns, letters to the editor, Q&As, pie charts and graphics, and/or interviews.

- Knows how to write clearly and in terse style—or knows enough to hand the work over to an editor.

- Expects to juggle the myriad tasks of running a business from the beginning.

- Realizes there is a group of people who wants to read what you have to say—and they're willing to pay money for it.

In addition, you need to be confident with making decisions that may later turn out to be mistakes, because even the *New York Times* prints retractions and corrections everyday. And though it's difficult—because after all, your business is your baby—you should try not to take it personally when a reader writes to disagree with something you wrote in the last issue, or cancels his or her subscription because of it. Of course you can concede when you're handed a particularly deft barb or comment, but if you want everyone to like you, you're in the wrong business. Frankly, I can't think of any business where you would be universally admired.

Anyway, stand your ground while you listen to your readers. Many newsletter publishers find that this is frequently a fine line to walk.

## Assessing Your Financial Goals

If you want to get rich, go buy a book by Charles Givens. If you want to have a decent income while you build equity and increase your revenues a bit each year, then keep reading.

To see if your financial goals jive with publishing a newsletter, ask yourself the following questions:

- What would you rather have after ten years of hard work: A large sum of money in the bank, or equity in a valuable business that would be relatively easy to sell?
- What's the least amount of money you could live on each month, provided that the mortgage, taxes, and utilities are paid for?
- Do you like doing just one thing to make a living, or do you prefer to juggle a variety of tasks?

For most people who decide to publish a newsletter, initially, money is usually a secondary concern. Of course, it takes money to get a newsletter up and running no matter who your audience is, but most people who get into the business are looking for the lifestyle and prestige first and income second. These priorities will help keep you motivated during the times when the money is slow.

After the uncertainties of the first year of publishing your newsletter, it will seem like you can relax a little once subscriptions come in a bit more regularly and revenue becomes more predictable, but you'll still find it necessary to reinvest much of the money back into the business in order to keep your revenue growing. Because of this, unless you have other means of income, you must learn to live frugally and get used to the idea of being cash-poor, at least for awhile. In time, most newsletter publishers learn to see this aspect of the business as a benefit. Publishing a newsletter provides them with knowledge, experience, and a reputation that they couldn't get any other way.

Many people who would like to start publishing a newsletter shy away from it for financial reasons. They can't see risking part of their hard-earned savings or paycheck in a business that may or may not make any money for them. Publishing a newsletter is all about financial risk, at least in the beginning. The possible payoff is great and the financial success will come your way if you stick with an idea that is popular with a segment of the public. Therefore, if you want to have a good income, or even a great one, go ahead and publish a newsletter. If you'd rather play it tried-and-true and feel safer with your money in a CD or savings account, then don't. There will be days when things are going to be hairy. In the end, however, you'll reach your financial goals publishing a newsletter with no problem.

## Assessing Your Tolerance for Risk

Many people who dream of publishing their own newsletter may love the idea and constantly fantasize about it. When it comes right down to it, most will never take the necessary steps because they're reluctant to leave the security of a regular job, health insurance, the familiarity of a particular lifestyle—you name it—even if they're unhappy in their current lives. A person who falls into this category has a low tolerance for risk of any kind.

On the other hand, if you can tolerate risk, even welcome it to some degree, and recognize that even though everything necessary is done to operate and promote the business, there is still an element of risk that any one person is unable to control, like economic downturns and fickle weather, than you are right for this business. Accepting this as a normal part of doing business, you can proceed accordingly.

What's your tolerance for risk? Find out by answering the following questions:

- Have you ever run a business of your own before? If so, how did you react when things slowed down? If you don't have experience in running a business, how do you think you would react—with panic, or the ability to constantly keep the big picture in mind?

- How would you react if you or a family member had to spend a week in the hospital and you didn't have health insurance because you needed the money to pay the mortgage?

People who don't have a high tolerance for risky situations often see the world in black and white, with no room for gray areas. Sure, the prospect of quitting your job or cutting back to part-time and starting to publish a newsletter is frightening even to people who like some excitement. There's no safety net; what makes you think you can pull this off; and what if you fail? are probably only three of the concerns that are running through your head before you decide to start your business. However, men and women who are able to see these factors as challenges to meet and surpass, and who like the absence of a schedule—as well as not knowing what the next day or week will bring—should be able to deal well with the unpredictable nature of the business.

Sometimes, in order to get into the business, it's necessary to do without the things you treasure. Many people finance their newsletter by selling family heirlooms, cars, even their homes, when there's no guarantee they'll be able to succeed. If you place great importance on your possessions and hate the idea of essentially gambling with their value, you should think twice about spending a lot of money to start publishing your newsletter, or else find someone else to finance it.

## Tools and Equipment You Will Need

I hear of many newsletter publishers who start their business with the latest, greatest and most expensive of everything. Admittedly, it's hard not to be dazzled by top-of-the-line computers, printers, fax machines, copiers, software, and other accoutrements you'll need to get before you even write the first word of the first article in the first issue of your newsletter. But time and again, I see people with a large credit line and the desire to have the best of everything go totally overboard when it comes to equipping their office. Even if they have the credit, it means they'll have to pull money that could be plowed into the business away from it in order to make a large interest payment on a credit card or loan.

"I'll grow into it," is how others justify buying a lot of expensive equipment that they don't need. Yes, but your expenses may be so high from the outset that your business may fail before it even has a chance to "grow into it."

It's entirely possible to equip your office with everything you need for about $2,000, at the time of this writing. Of course, this assumes that you won't be buying top-of-the-line anything, but functional items that serve their purpose and that you can easily upgrade—or pass on to an assistant—a year or two later.

In addition, to keep start-up costs down, you may decide to rent some of these tools or use an outside service—like a copy shop's fax machine and number—to save money. But I've found in the long run that you're better off buying a fax or learning how to lay out and insert copy into your newsletter yourself. Not only will you have more control over your newsletter, but you'll save time running to the copy shop, dropping off camera-ready proofs, and waiting for somebody else's schedule to free up.

Here is a list of the equipment that I find is necessary to publish a successful newsletter:

## Computers

You'll need a computer that can handle graphics programs—like a desktop publishing program. As the hardware becomes faster and more advanced, the prices will continue to drop. A year after I bought my 486/25 MHz computer with a SVGA monitor, 340 megabyte hard drive, loaded with software and a fax modem, I could buy a computer that's twice as fast with extras like a CD-ROM for the same money. You can skimp on the name brand—not everyone needs the perceived security and value of an IBM or Macintosh— but not on the machine's capability or storage space because you'll probably have to upgrade them sooner rather than later if you keep all of your business records, correspondence, and designed and finished newsletters on the computer. For instance, my computer has 4 mg RAM, and some of the programs I'd like to run require 8 mg RAM. So unless I upgrade to 8 mg of RAM for a couple of hundred bucks—again, as of this writing—I can't use the new versions of Quark or PageMaker, two of the most powerful and versatile desktop publishing programs. (If all of these letters and number combinations are like a foreign language to you, start hanging out at your local computer store or ask a salesman who knows what a computer could do for your business. Also start reading the computer magazines—especially *Home Office Computing.* They're filled with tips to help make your computer and your business run more smoothly.)

Some computers have fax modems and voice mail capabilities built into them, but most require that you keep the computer on all the time in order to receive faxes, while others require that you stop what you're working on when a fax comes in and switch to another program. I recommend a stand-alone fax with a dedicated line for any newsletter publisher. See my recommendations under Fax Machines and Phone Systems for more information.

**CD-ROM.** Try to get a computer with a built-in CD-ROM player. Software that's produced on CDs can hold ten times as much information as a floppy disk—which means a larger number of fonts to choose from on your desktop program. In addition, software on CD is usually priced the same—or less—as a program on floppy disk.

## Software

You'll need software to create your newsletter, keep track of your finances, and write your correspondence and articles. Most people have a personal preference—many times, it's the first word-processing program they learned how to use, which means there are a lot of people out there working on software that is both painfully obsolete and no longer serves their purpose.

Some people swear by Macintosh while others swear at it and prefer their Windows or DOS systems. Ask around and try a few different programs out—many software companies will send free sample disks of their programs where you can try before you buy.

For a newsletter publisher who is both new to computers and newsletter design, I'd recommend Microsoft Works for Windows—with word processing, database, and spreadsheet programs—and Microsoft Publisher, which provides you with professionally designed newsletter templates where all you have to do is plug in the text. For more advanced design, I'd recommend Quark or Ventura, which is now included as part of Corel Draw, a font and clipart program that provides more choices than you'll probably need in a lifetime.

## Printers

You could have the best computer and software in the world, but without a decent printer, your newsletter will be mud. Printers have gone through as much or even more changes than computers, starting out with dot matrix and daisy wheel printers, then proceeding to inkjet, bubble jet, and laser printers. If you're publishing a newsletter that people are paying good money for, I feel that nothing less than a laser printer will suffice. Laser printers can handle a larger variety of fonts and print clearer, crisper letters than the other kinds of printers. Try to get one that prints at least 300 dpi (dots per inch). Better yet, if you can spring for it, go for 600 dpi.

## Phone with a Built-In Answering Machine

I've gone through more than my fair share of answering machines over the years, and I've found that a combination phone and answering machine with redial, mute, flash, and memo features serves my purposes well. When I interview people for articles for my newsletters, I press a button and our conversation is instantly recorded. Of course, an answering machine is optional if you have an answering service or use voice mail features that are offered inexpensively through the phone company. But I prefer to have everything in my office where I don't have to call out in order to get my messages.

## Fax Machines and Phone Systems

Once I bought my fax machine and had it hooked up to its own separate line, I said what anyone who's discovered the benefits of a new piece of technology says, "I don't know how I lived without it for so long."

A fax machine is necessary to conduct business these days, if only because everyone else has them and has become overly reliant on them. There are a variety of options to choose from. Personally, I recommend staying away from the plain paper fax, spend your money on something else. If you want to convey the idea that you're running a serious business, I'd recommend that you have a separate line for your fax machine. Even though I have a business line for my main number, my second line—my fax machine—can be a residential line, which saves half the cost of a business line. But my fax line actually has two other numbers on it, both to answer incoming calls.

Keep in mind that if you want to reap the revenue that other professional newsletter publishers do, you must first act like a real business. Otherwise, both your subscribers and the people you interview for your newsletter—as well as suppliers and your creditors—won't treat you as a real business.

In my eyes, this means that anyone calling through to you should not have to be subjected to call-waiting or a busy signal. Also, a professional newsletter publisher should not have a device that tells the caller to press the pound sign to send a fax. Again, unfortunately, a precedent has been set. Most other businesses have dedicated fax lines, and so should you.

Voice mail through private systems and offered by the phone company automatically processes any call that comes in while you're already on the other line. But not where I live.

So after many fits and starts, I decided to have call-forwarding put on my line. Now, when someone calls in and I'm on the first line, the call gets forwarded to the fax line, where I've hooked up another answering machine. But even though the fax machine says it can differentiate between an incoming fax call and a call that goes to the answering machine, not all answering machines work with the fax. Mine didn't.

On to Round 3. I ordered RingMate from the phone company—a service where one line can have up to four different numbers, each with its own distinctive ring—and I hooked up a device that can send the incoming call to the appropriate machine based on the ring. So I still have my dedicated fax line. But when I'm on my first line and another call comes in, it gets forwarded to the first RingMate line, where an answering machine picks it up.

## Copy Machine

This not a necessity if you only make a few copies a week and can rely on the copy function in your fax machine to serve in a pinch until you can get to the copy shop. However, some newsletter publishers who send out a lot of regular press mailings say they couldn't live without a copy machine in their office.

Like other electronic business machines, the price of desktop copy machines has dropped drastically in recent years. If you check the newspapers, businesses that are going out of business can let top-of-the-line professional high-capacity machines sell for a fraction of their new prices.

## Other Equipment

The rest of the equipment you'll need is up to you, in terms of your personal preferences about desk, chair, storage units, bookcases, and other pieces of furniture. If you visit your local chain stationery store, you'll probably see a lot of things that you want but can probably do without right now, like the free-standing label machine, the automatic letter folding and stuffing machine, and the binding device for those specialized workbooks you're thinking of developing in the future. Browse through the store so you know what's out there. It may even give you some ideas for other ancillary products, but until your subscription numbers grow, sit tight. There's nothing worse than developing a new product for a market that doesn't yet exist.

Just remember to go slowly at first, get as much as you need and can afford and then grow with it. You'll know when it's time to upgrade.

## Financial Requirements

As I mentioned in the section on the different types of equipment you'll need to start publishing your newsletter, you can get started by spending about $2,000. But that's just to fully equip your office with the communications technology you'll need. In one sense, it's only the beginning.

In order to attract subscribers to your newsletter, you'll have to spend money promoting it in a variety of ways, such as direct mail, advertising, and publicity, to let the media and public know that you exist. It's easy to spend too much money on promotion that is ineffective and untargeted in the beginning while you're still fine-tuning who your audience actually is. We'll get into the nitty gritty of marketing, estimating your annual marketing costs, and testing what works best for you in Chapter 7. With a newsletter, maybe more than with any other business, it's likely that the single largest expense in your budget will be marketing expenses, which includes part or most of your phone, postage, and printing bills.

You'll need to hook up a phone and budget for initial pro-motional mailings, and sending out sample issues. The cost of starting to publish a newsletter can vary widely, depending upon the vision you have of your newsletter, and whether you want to grow your subscription list quickly or if you're content to go slowly. If you're thinking about buying an existing news-letter you'll inevitably spend more than if you were to start from scratch. Then again, if the asking price of an existing newsletter you're thinking of buying seems ridiculously low, then you're right to be suspicious since you're supposedly pur-chasing a going business with a built-in customer list and a good reputation. Starting from scratch means less revenue in the beginning, but also less expense to get started.

I hesitate to give exact figures for expenses, since I know there are people out there who have spent much less and also those who splurged. For *Sticks* I bought my computer system, added a fax and complex phone system and spent about $750 to publicize the first issue, which included ads, printing, post-age, and phone bills. I later financed marketing programs with the revenue that was generated by the first mailing.

Because many people are eager to start their businesses right away, they choose to spend more money at the outset so they can start making money right away. If you have the patience and the cash to support yourself until your newsletter is up and running, with a healthy renewal rate—which usually takes several years to develop—then I think it's always better to take your time.

## The Skills You'll Need

Certainly as a newsletter publisher, the ability to write clearly as well as speak clearly—to convey your message to both the media and to prospective subscribers—is important to your success. If you know that you're lacking in these areas, you'll be able to find someone who can handle these reins for you and also serve as a spokesperson. Though many newsletter publishers resist this from the outset, others embrace it so they can concentrate on running and growing their business to the level they desire.

After years of experience from publishing five different newsletters, I can tell you that the most important skill you can have in this business is the ability to keep one eye focused on the seemingly endless details involved in producing and promoting a regular publication while keeping the other eye fixed on your long-term goals. This is not an easy thing to achieve, and indeed, there are many times when I find myself veering off too far in one direction, spending a few days thinking about how I'm going to add 500 more subscribers in the next six months with nary a thought about the articles that are going into the next issue, which is due at the printer next week. If you're a born juggler, you'll probably find yourself in the same situation from time to time. Because you may not mind doing the grunt work—again, it is your baby—and because stuffing envelopes and entering names and addresses into your database of potential subscribers gives you a break from the hard work of planning, writing, and editing articles, you may sometimes find yourself doing *too* much grunt work. The opposite may happen, too.

Other skills that you'll need fall under the category of running a business, which any new entrepreneur can learn about from the variety of books on how to start a business. You'll need to learn about cash flow, bookkeeping, and marketing, but again you can usually learn as you go. You can also ask other newsletter publishers what business methods have worked best for them.

Even if you've never run a business before, you probably already know what you're good at from working for other people. And where your skills aren't as good, you'll be able to learn enough to get by. If you can afford to hire someone else to do some of the work, go ahead.

## Attitude Requirements

In my eyes, the ideal person to publish a newsletter is someone who's a cynical optimist, or, as some might say, an optimistic cynic. This is a person who has a positive attitude toward the world, but who also is not terribly surprised when things go wrong. When that happens, you spring into action and do whatever it takes to address the problem and get everything back to normal—until the next time.

As a newsletter publisher, you'll be dealing with a variety of people and situations as well as a business, that is, in essence, operating 24 hours a day—at least in your mind. As a result, surprises will come up from time to time, especially in the beginning. As long as you maintain a positive attitude and remain alert to problems that need your immediate attention while learning patience for those that can wait, you'll be able to successfully publish a newsletter and maintain your equilibrium as well. And remember, at least once a week, you should take a few hours to get away from the business, especially if you work from a home office; this will help you maintain your positive attitude as well.

Perhaps the most important aspect of your attitude you'll need to publish a newsletter is a firm fixation on your business as well as a strong belief in your subject. This, more than any other part of your personality, will give you what it takes when you're dealing with subscribers and potential customers, as well as those times when you need a heavy dose of motivation to pull you through any lulls you may experience.

## Your Assets and Liabilities

Before you start working on the first issue of your newsletter, it's a good idea to analyze your assets and liabilities—personal, financial, and those that involve your house, if you choose to work from home.

Starting up any business is rough. Publishing a newsletter can be especially hard because you will be throwing out your thoughts, ideas, and advice, and rarely getting any feedback, either favorable or not. Think about it: whenever you read an article that provokes you—either positively or negatively—do you immediately sit down and write a letter to the editor? Probably not. Unsolicited feedback will usually come several issues down the road, and then only in a trickle. However, if you want feedback before that, you will have to ask for it. Why not call some of your readers and ask what they do and don't like, and what kind of articles they'd like to see?

Living in the same place where you work can also present a strain. People who run other types of home-based businesses find that one solution is to close the door to their office to take a break. Nevertheless, a home-based business will affect your entire family. How will you and your family cope with the adjustment? Good communication and developing a plan in advance to share some private downtime together each day, is a definite asset and will help prioritize your goals about publishing a newsletter.

As for money, experts always say you should budget at least twice as much as you think you need. By the way, the same philosophy also applies to the amount of time you'll need to get your business up and running. In terms of money, you'll need a financial cushion of several thousand dollars to cover both unexpected business and personal expenses at the very least, and financial experts usually recommend much more than this figure. There are always extra expenses that come up that you hadn't budgeted for, or an emergency will arise that requires an immediate infusion of cash like renting a booth at a trade show or a special deal on an ad in a trade publication. The important thing to know is that your liabilities can be addressed quickly if you have the assets—that is, the extra cash—to fix them as soon as possible.

## Action Guidelines

✔ Take some time to decide if you're right for the newsletter publishing business—and if the business is right for you.

✔ Evaluate whether the slow and steady financial growth of most newsletters matches up with your personal goals.

✔ If you don't have the stomach for risk-taking, lay in a big supply of Maalox if you're determined to publish a newsletter.

✔ Make a list of the tools and equipment you'll need in order to publish your newsletter.

✔ Figure out how much money you'll need to start.

✔ Decide which tasks you'll assume based on your own skills.

## Newsletter Publisher Profile

### Ron Rich
### *Booktalk*

Ron Rich had been an elementary school teacher and principal for 30 years. He had developed a reputation as an expert in children's literature and frequently gave talks on children's books in his classrooms.

He took an early retirement in 1990. At first he didn't know what he was going to do. When he voiced his concerns to a friend, the friend replied, "I'm sure it will have something to do with children's books." He turned out to be right.

"I wanted to publish a newsletter about books geared toward kids from kindergarten through the eighth grade," recalls Rich. The result is *Booktalk,* an eight-page newsletter containing reviews of recently published books. When he started the newsletter in 1991, Rich initially geared it toward teachers and parents. He quickly discovered librarians are the ones who have the money to buy the books and who want to know what's new in the field, so he began to promote *Booktalk* primarily to them.

He publishes the newsletter monthly from September through June and charges $32.50. School districts frequently pay for the subscriptions. In 1993 he had 100 subscribers, but hopes to increase his circulation to 500. He reinvests all the money he receives back into promotion and direct mail.

To market the newsletter, Rich sends flyers to school libraries. He also attends state book conferences, frequently as a speaker. Another service he's developed is a program for kindergarten through 6th grade called, Let's Read A Book. He visits school classes and reads to the class in 30-minute sessions. In 1992 Rich conducted 20 such sessions.

Rich works as the Children's Reading Specialist in the local Barnes & Noble bookstore; he also manages the children's department, with over 12,000 titles. He likes working at the bookstore particularly because he has access to any title he'd like to read. He often is visited by subscribers to his newsletter.

Rich spends about 20 hours a week working on the newsletter. He gets his books from the news releases and review copies that publishers send him; he also reads new titles from the store. Since he already had a computer, he spent very little on the first issue. "I started with 500 names; they were names of acquaintances, people I was working with and people at school districts. I sent each a copy of the first issue, which I mailed first class," he recalls. Half of his subscribers live in Colorado, with the rest scattered through 29 other states.

"It's a one-person business, and I do it all myself," he remarks. "This is not stressful, it's real enjoyment." The only downside is that with a subscription-only publication, many people don't renew. "I have to constantly campaign about my cause to replace the readers who don't renew," he indicates. Every year the number of those who do renew is increasing.

Currently Rich is exploring how to expand the newsletter to include parents who don't have the funds to buy new books that librarians do, since the average children's book costs $15. "I think some parents who subscribe to *Booktalk* use the newsletter to identify certain books, and then check them out of the libraries," he says.

"Publishing the newsletter gives me a lot of personal satisfaction and forces me to keep on top of things," though he admits with 5,000 to 6,000 new children's books published each year, it can be difficult. "Be prepared not to make a lot of money in the beginning," he advises. "Do your homework in identifying your audience, because if this is going to be a career for you, make sure it's going to be fun and profitable."

# NEWSLETTER
# RESOURCES

W hen you first get your idea for the type of newsletter you'd like to publish, and begin to think about making it a reality, be prepared for the possibility that you may feel utterly alone. After all, starting a business is a big change for many people, and even though you may have the greatest of expectations, the truth is that at this point you really don't know how your idea will take off.

You should realize, however, that you have plenty of company, and that you have the benefit of the information that other people have gathered before you, both through their mistakes as well as their successes. And not only is there a wealth of information about the industry, but there are specific things you have to know when you set up your business, and it's all relatively easy to gather. In addition, there are specific suppliers who specialize in providing newsletter publishers with the products, services, and advice you'll need to truly make your newsletter business as individual as you are.

## Using Your Own—and Others'—Experiences

When it comes time to start to utilize the vast array of resources that are available to help you start publishing your newsletter, one of the best ways to begin is to dive headfirst into it all. You have a pretty good idea of the topic of your newsletter by now, and undoubtedly an opinion on that topic. However, at the same time, you should be aware of the many experts, resources, and groups you can draw on to help make the content of your newsletter as strong as it can be.

When I started my newsletter *Travel Marketing Bulletin*, I did what I suggested you do in Chapter 1. I sat down and made a list of 100 article ideas. For this, I drew on my own marketing techniques that have worked in the past as well as the problems I faced, whether I solved them or not.

But I also drew on the experience of the many owners of small travel businesses that I had talked with over the years when I wrote travel articles for magazines and newspapers. I called them up and asked them about their marketing problems, what they'd like to see more information on, and other topics. Their answers helped me to refine my list of 100 ideas and I added more article ideas as well.

Though many, but not all, newsletters have an advisory board, I decided to form one for *Travel Marketing Bulletin*. The purpose of an advisory board is to add credibility to the newsletter as well as form a group of experts who I could call upon for advice and suggestions. When I assembled my advisory board, I looked for a cross-section of small travel business owners, most of whom had some specific expertise in marketing. I selected an innkeeper who had gotten her inn written up in most of the coveted magazines, the owner of a large western travel clearinghouse who booked tourists on everything from dude ranch vacations to llama packing trips, and a woman who served as communications director for a small California winery whose aim was to attract tourists for the winery tours.

I provide all of the members of my advisory board with a free subscription to the newsletter. Every few months I call each of them up and ask what they think of the newsletter, and solicit new story ideas. They also provide me with the latest news from their respective industries. Sometimes I publish the information in the newsletter; other times, I just file it away.

Some of the larger newsletters pay their advisory board members a stipend in exchange for meeting once a year, usually during an annual trade conference that the majority of people in the business attend. I don't think this is entirely necessary, especially when you're first starting out. As long as you let your advisory board promote the fact that they're important enough to have been selected for the board, and that they can use their membership on the board as a way to further their own careers, that's usually enough for them. A big reason for why I have an advisory board, however, is that it gives my newsletter a stamp of approval whenever I include their names, companies, and their accomplishments in my promotional materials. Similar to when I include quotes and media endorsements that I've picked up along the way. Even though the person who receives my direct mail letter may not have heard of any of the members of my board, the fact that I have an advisory board at all is enough to impress.

## Trade Associations

As is often said, it's not what you know, it's who you know. And membership in a variety of business associations can help you start your newsletter and get ahead. Joining a trade association when you're first starting out can be invaluable in terms of the contacts you can make as well as advice from people who have been publishing newsletters—or in the communications business in one form or another—for a long time. With the advent of desktop publishing, there are more newsletters being published today than ever before, which is reflected in the increased membership of the various organizations and the clout of the newsletter trade associations. In addition, organizations that focus on a variety of specific issues that you'll deal with in your business—direct marketing, advertising, publishing—exist both on a national and regional basis, with state chapters of the large organizations as well as individual specialty groups. For example, I belong to the Vermont/New Hampshire Direct Marketing Association, a group of professionals who both focus and dabble in direct marketing and who meet every six weeks for a luncheon, talks, discussion, and networking. I've found that these meetings bring the issues that are often frequent discussions in business magazines to life so that you can surmise whether they'll work for you.

I'd recommend you join an association that covers the industry you're exploring in your newsletter, in addition to applying for membership in one of the newsletter associations. Most associations publish a regular newsletter for their members, sell literature that covers specific aspects of the business, and hold occasional conventions where members can network with each other, attend workshops, and visit trade show exhibitors who sell products that are pertinent to the business. Some associations also offer their members consultation services at reduced rates, credit card acceptance privileges through a clearinghouse, and long-distance and toll-free number services at a discount. Though yearly membership rates can be high—sometimes up to $500 a year in some cases—most newsletter publishers report that it's worth it because of all the benefits, networking, and ideas they receive to help them enhance their own businesses.

In addition to the national trade associations, there are many regional, statewide, and local organizations that newsletter publishers can join as well. These usually benefit newsletter publishers by providing local marketing opportunities as well as a reliable source of feedback. For instance, some of the smaller associations are started by a group of local members of a particular national organization. They meet through the national association, talk regularly on their own, then decide to form their own chapter. And some newsletter publishers even start their own associations.

## National Associations

The two major national newsletter publishing associations are The Newsletter Association, and The Newsletter Clearinghouse. The Newsletter Association serves as a nonprofit trade association for newsletter publishers, offering a semi-monthly newsletter, regular meeting opportunities, seminars, and an annual conference. The Newsletter Clearinghouse also publishes a newsletter about newsletter publishing, another about newsletter design, conducts regular seminars and workshops, and provides more customized information, offering it on an a la carte basis instead. You can write to each group for more information:

The Newsletter Association
1401 Wilson Blvd., Suite 207
Arlington, VA 22209
703-527-2333

The Newsletter Clearinghouse
44 W. Market St.
Rhinebeck, NY 12572
914-876-2081

You also shouldn't overlook the local, regional, and state communication and publishing associations for information and networking opportunities in your area.

## Consultants

Almost as quickly as new newsletters have been popping up all over the country, there has been a bevy of consultants to help novice newsletter publishers do their homework before they start a publication of their own. These same professionals can then help fledgling newsletter publishers learn how to publish through attendance at conventions, seminars, or one-on-one meetings. In many cases, the people who work as consultants have also published newsletters of their own, either now or in the past, so they have plenty of first-hand experience to draw on and help steer their clients toward the best situation. Some consultants will also hook you up with a newsletter where you can work as an intern to see if you really want to pursue publishing one of your own.

New seminars and conventions for aspiring and experienced newsletter publishers are scheduled on a regular basis. The best way to find one in your area is to check the notices and advertisements in the newsletters published by the national and regional newsletter and communications associations, as well as the independent publications for the trade.

Here's a partial list of consultants who may or may not also serve as convention and seminar organizers:

Padgett-Thompson
11221 Roe Ave.
Leawood, KS 66211
800-255-4141 or 913-451-2900

Dynamic Graphics Educational Foundation
6000 North Forest Park Dr.
Peoria, IL 61614
800-255-8800 or 309-688-8866

Williams Hill Communications
RR 1, Box 1234
Grafton, NH 03240
800-639-1099 or 603-523-7877

The Newsletter Factory
1640 Powers Ferry Rd., Bldg. 8 #110
Marietta, GA 30067
404-955-2002

## Training Courses

Many of the convention organizers mentioned previously also hold special workshops solely for prospective newsletter publishers. I've also seen community colleges, adult schools, and even computer centers include newsletter publishing courses on their regular schedule. However, you should realize that not only will people like you attend, with an eye toward publishing a newsletter for profit, but also employees in charge of publishing their company newsletters, as well as members of social groups who have been designated to handle the task of producing a newsletter. Even though some of the topics covered in these seminars may not entirely apply to you and your newsletter, it's still a good idea to attend all the classes; you may get a few ideas for your own newsletter that you may not have previously considered.

To find out about future courses, you should write to the organizers and ask to be placed on their mailing list so you can be alerted to upcoming workshops and seminars. Most courses that don't take place within a community school format will last a few intensive days, and will provide you with a condensed birds-eye view of the business. Some involve strictly sit-down classroom learning, while others require you to create a newsletter as well as your business plan over the course of a few days. This kind of workshop usually begins on a Friday and doesn't let up until the participants collapse Sunday afternoon.

Here are some of the groups and companies that offer courses in the rudiments of newsletter publishing:

Editorial Experts
85 South Bragg St.
Alexandria, VA 22312
703-683-0683

Performance Seminar Group
325 Myrtle Ave.
Bridgeport, CT 06604
203-335-3023

Pattison Workshops
5092 Kingscross Rd.
Westminster, CA 92683
714-894-8143

Promotional Perspectives
1955 Pauline Blvd., #100A
Ann Arbor, MI 48103
313-994-0007

Ragan Communications
407 South Dearborn St.
Chicago, IL 60605
312-922-8245

## Books

Though this book will provide you with everything you need to know to plan and publish your newsletter, there is a significant amount of specific information published by independent publishers and newsletter organizations designed to help newsletter publishers to navigate the stickier aspects of publishing a newsletter.

Following is a list of titles that will help newsletter publishers run their businesses more profitably:

Arth, Marvin, and Ashmore, Helen. *Newsletter Editor's Desk Book*, 4th Edition. St Louis: Newsletter Resources, 1994.

Beach, Mark. *Editing Your Newsletter.* Cincinnati: Writer's Digest Books, 1988.

Floyd, Elaine. *Copy-Ready Forms for Newsletters.* St Louis: Newsletter Resources, 1994.

Floyd, Elaine. *Making Money Writing Newsletters.* St Louis: Newsletter Resources, 1994.

Floyd, Elaine. *Marketing With Newsletters.* St Louis: Newsletter Resources, 1991.

Floyd, Elaine. *Quick & Easy Newsletters on a Shoestring Budget.* St Louis: Newsletter Resources, 1994.

Goss, Frederick. *Success in Newsletter Publishing.* Arlington, VA: Newsletter Association, 1985.

Hudson, Howard Penn. *Publishing Newsletters.* New York: Scribners, 1988.

## Newsletter Directories

*Investment Newsletters*
Larimi Communications
246 W. 38 St.
New York, NY 10018

*The National Directory of Investment Newsletters*
Idea Publishing Corporation
55 E. Afton Ave.
Yardley, PA 19067

*Newsletter Yearbook Directory*
The Newsletter Clearinghouse
44 West Market St.
Rhinebeck, NY 12572

*Newsletters Directory*
Gale Research
Book Tower
Detroit, MI 48226

*Oxbridge Directory of Newsletters*
150 Fifth Ave., #301
New York, NY 10011

## Magazines and Trade Journals

Again, many of the newsletter publishing and other trade associations I've mentioned publish specialized newsletters that address the many topics that concern their members, as well as insight into how recently passed legislation and tax information will affect the industry in the future. There are independent journals as well. Here are some of these:

*Newsletter News & Resources*
Newsletter Resources
6614 Pernod Ave.
St Louis, MO 63139
800-264-6305

*The Newsletter on Newsletters*
The Newsletter Clearinghouse
44 West Market St.
Rhinebeck, NY 12572
914-876-2081

*Newsletter Design*
The Newsletter Clearinghouse
44 West Market St.
Rhinebeck, NY 12572
914-876-2081

## Suppliers

In my opinion, the most important supplier you will be dealing with is your printer. I prefer to work with a local printer so that I can inspect the final printed materials and catch any errors before they are sent out to subscribers.

Through trial and error, you will find the printer who works best with your business. Be forewarned that printing prices can vary as much as 500 percent on the same job, so shop around and ask to see samples of previous newsletters that a particular printer has produced. The number of pieces you need to have printed will also influence your final decision on which printer to use. You may also find that while one printer will be ideal to print your newsletter, glossy four-color brochures and specialized mailings may require a large volume color printer that has special machines to give you the quality you're looking for. Again, you should shop around and if at all possible, ask to see a few samples from your actual run—they can be faxed—before the printer proceeds with the entire run.

Another "supplier" which will eventually provide you with an invaluable service is a mailing house. In the beginning, most newsletter publishers will opt to do the folding, labeling, stamping, and mailing themselves. As your subscription list grows, however, you'll find yourself cursing the time you'll have to spend on getting 500 newsletters out on time, not to mention the paper cuts. I've found that 500 is the magic cut-off number—below that, I can handle myself. Above that, with every envelope I stuff, it makes me think about the important stuff I could be doing, like marketing the business and making follow-up phone calls to editors who may write up my newsletter in their publication when prompted by a phone call by me. What you may want to do in lieu of hiring a mailing house is hire a neighbor or high school kid to come in—or take home—the envelopes to stuff in front of the TV.

A mailing service can also serve as your circulation department, handling all of your inquiries, entering new subscriptions on a computerized database, send you the checks, and mail out the newsletter. They can also sort it by zip code and send each issue out bulk rate, but I prefer to send my newsletter out first class. First of all, bulk rate is not the most reliable form of mail delivery, and second, especially with a higher-priced newsletter, subscribers feel that they're entitled to speedy delivery. Indeed, some business newsletter publishers are now offering a fax service so their subscribers won't feel they're receiving vital information after it's become old news.

Find your printer and mailing house through the recommendation of other local businesses, as well as your own impressions of their work.

## Small Business Administration

The Small Business Administration (SBA), which you help to pay for with your tax dollars, is a veritable gold mine of information if you want to start publishing your own newsletter. There are three major divisions within the SBA that can assist you in the start-up phase of your business, as well as provide you with advice and assistance once your newsletter business is up and running.

One is the Small Business Development Center (SBDC), which counsels entrepreneurs in every conceivable type of business and at every level of development. The SBDC will set you up in private sessions with an entrepreneur who has experience publishing a newsletter, or at least has hands-on experience in the communications industry. There, you can ask about any phase of publishing a newsletter that you'd like, from marketing to locating suitable financing, and how to keep the business going in tough times.

The SBA also runs the Small Business Institute (SBI) on a number of college campuses nationwide. Each SBI tends to specialize in a given field, from engineering to business management, but if you're looking for very specific information, contact the nearest SBI that has the program you want. The assistance at an SBI is largely provided by students in the program, but always under the watchful eye of a professor or administrator.

SCORE, or the Service Corps of Retired Executives, can be an exciting place for you to get information about your business. SCORE officers provide one-on-one counseling with retired business people who volunteer their time to help entrepreneurs like you get the help you need. All the volunteer counselors have extensive experience in a particular field and are eager to share their insights. SCORE also offers a variety of seminars and workshops on all aspects of business ownership that aspiring newsletter publishers can also attend; here, you'll get specific advice about the nuts and bolts of running a business in general, from bookkeeping to taxes.

The Small Business Administration also has a program where it loans money to small businesses, but you have to apply through a bank. The SBA then kicks in some of the funds and serves to guarantee your loan based on your business plan. The SBA also offers a large variety of helpful booklets and brochures on all aspects of running a business.

To locate the SBA and its other programs, look in the white pages of the phone book under United States Government. Call the office nearest you for information about the programs and services they provide locally. To contact the SBA in Washington directly, write to them at:

The Small Business Administration
409 Third St., SW
Washington, DC 20416

To get in touch with the variety of services, call the SBA Answer Desk at 800-827-5722 for immediate help; or go online with the SBA at 800-697-4636

## Organizations that Help Small Business

Once you start publishing your newsletter, you'll be joining the millions of other Americans who are owning and operating their own small businesses. Specific questions can pop up, and you'll undoubtedly want to network with other entrepreneurs who aren't necessarily in the same field in order to get your questions answered.

There are a number of nationwide associations that provide small business owners with information, specific resources, discounts on business products and services, and the ability to work with other members. The government also gets into the act.

Here's a listing of a number of nationwide organizations that have proven to be valuable to the entrepreneurs who join them.

National Association for the Self-Employed
PO Box 612067
Dallas, TX 75261
800-232-6273

National Association of Home Based Businesses
10451 Mill Run Circle, Suite 400
Owings Mills, MD 21117
410-363-3698

National Federation of Independent Business
600 Maryland Ave., SW, Suite 700
Washington, DC 20024
202-554-9000

American Woman's Economic Development Corporation
71 Vanderbilt Ave., Suite 320
New York, NY 10169
800-222-2933

National Association of Women Business Owners
1377 K St., NW, Suite 637
Washington, DC 20005
301-608-2590

National Minority Business Council
235 E. 42 St.
New York, NY 10017
212-573-2385

## Action Guidelines

✔ Use your own experiences to set the tone for your newsletter. This is what will attract readers to your newsletter.

✔ Join one or more trade associations to network and learn where to get the information you need.

✔ Contact some newsletter publishing consultants for expert advice, or take a few courses.

✔ Subscribe to a few trade journals and newspapers.

✔ Get in touch with the Small Business Administration for specialized business advice.

### Newsletter Publisher Profile

### Marie Kiefer
### *Book Promotion Hotline*

Book publishers are a lot like newsletter publishers: they must spend a good deal of their time marketing their publications. Back in 1987, John Kremer, a book publisher with a knack for marketing, saw that other book publishers needed help in the form of advice and marketing contacts. So he started a publication called *Book Marketing Update*, at the time a bimonthly newsletter that was filled with information to help book publishers promote their books more effectively.

One of his employees, Marie Kiefer, helped him to get *BMU* up and running. He soon felt that his readers needed even more market information, they needed it quickly, and more often than once every two months. So he decided to start *Book Promotion Hotline*, a weekly four-page newsletter that is information-based, in that it gives just the contact information—the names and phone numbers of editors at publications and producers at TV and radio stations—and leaves it up to the book publisher—his subscribers—to contact them.

In the interim, John's company, Ad-Lib Publications, bumped *Book Marketing Update* up to ten issues a year in 1994 and sold the company to Marie. Part of the arrangement is that John still publishes, edits and promotes *BMU* while Marie is responsible for *BPH*, among other projects at Ad-Lib, such as a catalog of books of interest to publishers as well as market databases and Special Reports. John's reason for selling the company was to focus more on consulting and publishing his own books under his own imprint—Open Horizons—but the two companies pass along contact information and also do a good deal of cross-promotion of the other company's products.

*Book Promotion Hotline* costs $150 a year, which is comparable to several other weekly media placement newsletters. Marie reports that the newsletter's current circulation is about 150. She has a staff of three full-timers and three part-timers who research the leads and check accuracy. In each issue, there will be information about newspapers, magazines, TV, or radio shows. Many of the publishers who subscribe to the newsletter use it to update their media information on the media Data Files that they've purchased through Ad-Lib. Says Marie: "That's why we like to concentrate on listing more media in each issue, since that's where most of the changes occur." *BPH* also lists bookstores and catalog companies that sell books. In fact, any place that you could publicize or sell a book can be included in *BPH*, according to Marie. However, she does have a few subscribers who are not publishers and who use the information to promote other products.

To get new subscribers to *BPH*, Marie tries to mail out a direct mail package to about 500 publishers every other week or so. Her in-house prospect list contains about 17,000 names, and she gets new names by reading the industry trade publications for news about new businesses. She works hard to keep her mailing list up to date. She also plans to start doing some publicity to promote the newsletter; as her husband told her recently, "You're doing the work anyway, you might as well have more subscribers."

Marie likes publishing a newsletter because she gets to talk to many different people in the business from all over the country. She says that the hardest part is setting aside the time to write the newsletter; she admits that she tends to do the writing—which takes about six or seven hours—at night and on the weekend when the phone doesn't ring incessantly. The research takes approximately two days, and her staff handles this task.

The ironic part of *BPH* is that the newsletter contains so much information that some people just can't keep up. "A lot of people actually discontinue their subscription because there's too much in it, and too many leads for them," says Marie. "I'm staying with the current format, though, for the time being."

# *PLANNING YOUR NEWSLETTER BUSINESS*

P lanning is the key to the success of your newsletter. If you set out without it, I feel that you're basically setting out on a lengthy cross-country car trip without a map. You'll spend a good deal of time relying on the advice of other people to give you information on where to go and how to get there, instead of your own plans, dreams, and instincts.

This is why it's important that you take the time now to plan your newsletter down to the smallest detail. I believe it's the single most important thing you can do to ensure the success of your newsletter as well as other products and services that may spring from it.

## Planning to Succeed

Before starting a newsletter—or any business, for that matter—every entrepreneur *expects* to succeed. However, only a handful *plan* to succeed, and therein lies the difference.

Planning to succeed means you'll have to think about how you envision your newsletter, as well as writing a business plan and a marketing plan. Though many businesses do succeed without developing these planning materials, it's easier to plan to succeed if you take the time to plot out every aspect of your business, from the number of pages in each issue to your logo to even how you'll answer the phone.

Getting the details down in writing months—or years—before your first subscriber signs up will not only help to clarify your vision of your newsletter and your business, but it will also provide you with a blueprint to check every so often to see that you're on target and on schedule. If you're not, you'll be able to backtrack to discover why you've been delayed or else you may determine that your original plan was a bit too ambitious. As I've already said, take the time now to plan your business. Later on, it may be too late and lead to . . .

## Unplanned Failure

Even with the best of intentions and the most detailed business and marketing plans, sometimes a newsletter will fail, or at least seriously underperform the publisher's initial projections. Perhaps the expectations were overly optimistic or else their budget didn't allow for much leeway, which occurs frequently among new newsletter publishers until they become familiar with the rhythms of the operation. Sometimes events beyond your control can occur—like a prolonged downturn in the economy, or a lull in the growth of the industry that your newsletter covers—and nothing can be done to salvage even a well-written business plan.

The most common causes of unplanned failure among newsletter publishers are insufficient marketing and unfocused editorial direction. In the first instance, many newsletter publishers overestimate the initial enthusiasm from prospective subscribers. As I'll cover in the marketing chapter (Chapter 7), many times people need to see your name out there a number of times before they'll respond. And if you're a new business, others will tend to wait around a year before subscribing to make sure that you'll make it that long.

Unfocused editorial direction can also cause a newsletter to fail. For most newsletters there's usually a huge difference in quality between a newsletter's first issue and the first issue of the second year. It takes awhile to find your voice and strength in a newsletter, and hopefully by the end of the first year your newsletter has developed a positive reputation among the people you want to attract. I know that I try not to send out copies of my first and second issues of one of my newsletters for promotional purposes. From the vantage point of a year later, they seem sparse, cocky, and the articles seem to be unrelated to each other.

However, some newsletter publishers never get beyond those first tentative, slightly amateurish issues. Either the publisher and/or editor is blind to the product, or they are so wrapped up in the business end of things, the newsletter— which is the most important part of the business—is given short shift. Remember, readers don't care if you're keeping up with your business goals behind the scenes; they only care about the information that the newsletter contains. Like I've already said and will undoubtedly say a few more times, if you don't provide your readers with information they can use on a regular basis, they'll have no reason to subscribe or renew.

Lack of capital can also come into play, because even though most business and marketing plans do account for these factors, most people underestimate the amount of cash they'll need to pay the bills during slow times—which is most of the time in the beginning—as well as the amount of time they'll need to spend on marketing just to get their names out there and keep them there. Another reason that is rarely mentioned about why newsletters fail is because despite everything they read and all the workshops and seminars that they attend, most people still vastly underestimate the amount of time and energy it takes to publish a newsletter. Couples especially who run the business as a joint venture may be particularly surprised at the wedge the business can begin to drive into their relationship if they're not careful. In addition, they may have vastly different management styles that they weren't aware when they started the business.

As you're drawing up the three major ways to avoid unplanned failure—visualizing your newsletter, writing a business plan, and writing a marketing plan—try to stay aware of anything that causes little alarms to go off in your brain, like keeping only $1,000 in an emergency fund account, or when someone suggests it's a simple matter to get 2,000 subscribers in your first six months of business. You're right to stop, take a deep breath, and go for a walk. Listen to these warning signals and try to put some perspective into what it's like to publish a newsletter before you even start. The best way to avoid unplanned failure is if you can regard all income from the newsletter as money to plow back into the business, and not revenue you have to depend on to pay the mortgage and taxes. Of course, that means you might have to limit the number of subscription offers that you mail out each month while you or your partner—or both of you—are still working a full-time job. Many newsletter publishers who have been in the business awhile suggest that you start slowly and gradually expand the business. That way, the mistakes you make will still be manageable, and you won't flip out when no new subscriptions come in for an entire month, because you'll still have income—and savings.

## Visualizing Your Newsletter

Before you get into the nuts and bolts of writing a business and marketing plan for your newsletter, now is a perfect time to fantasize about exactly how you visualize your publication (see Figure 4.1). You may want to fill out this form twice: once

**Figure 4.1:**

### Newsletter Objectives

1. What do you think the best name for your newsletter should be?

   _____

   _____

2. How often will you publish each issue?

   _____

   _____

3. What will be the name of your company?

   _____

   _____

4. Will you publish your newsletter from your home or from an outside office? Will you devote yourself to it full- or part-time?

   _____

   _____

5. How many pages will each issue contain?

   _____

   _____

6. Write the table of contents for the first issue.

   _____

   _____

7. What type of people will read your newsletter?

   _____

   _____

**Figure 4.1 (*cont.*)**

8. Will you have photos in each issue? What about clip art?

9. Describe the design of your newsletter using other newsletters as examples.

10. How and where will you market your newsletter?

11. If you plan to hire an employee, what tasks will you assign?

12. What are some of the ancillary products you'd like to offer with the newsletter? What will their topics be?

13. What will be on your answering machine tape? Or will you hire an answering service?

14. What will make your newsletter stand out?

15. Who are your competitors? How will your newsletter be different?

for how you see your newsletter when you're first starting out, and again a year or more later, after you are able to gain some perspective and expertise on your topic and start to mold it into what you really want your newsletter to be for the long term. If you're starting your newsletter with a partner, both of you should separately fill out this form and compare your answers. If any of your answers are radically different, you should address them now to avoid unnecessary expense and disagreements later.

## Writing Your Business Plan

Why should you have a business plan? You know exactly what you're going to do—publish a newsletter. You know where it will be located, and when you want to do it. Even if your goals are not that specific at this point, you probably have an idea of the type of newsletter you'd like to publish.

Writing a business plan will help you to map out a specific blueprint for you to follow on your way to meeting your business goals. A business plan allows that there is no question about the smallest aspect of getting your newsletter off the ground; in the confusion and excitement, after all, many things get overlooked. Getting it all down in writing provides you with a detailed itinerary. And since you write the plan yourself, you'll be able to tailor it to your own needs, and also to tinker with it later when unforeseen roadblocks begin to emerge.

With a business plan in hand, you'll be able to show the bank, your suppliers, and other potential business contacts exactly how you visualize your newsletter, in language and figures they understand. But writing is a funny thing that reveals a lot as it unfolds. Not only will your business plan provide you with a broad picture of your business, in addition to allowing you to get all of the little details down in writing, but you'll also think of other things as you think, write, and plan aspects of your prospective business that might not have come up otherwise.

Having a business plan written before you do anything else for your newsletter will put you way ahead of your competition, since most businesses do not take the time before hand to plan out their strategies as carefully.

Although a business plan is vital to the successful start-up of a newsletter, you shouldn't tuck it away in a drawer and forget about it. It is meant to be used and referred to as you progress in your business. Periodically checking the progress you're making against the goals you put forth in the plan allow you to see where changes need to be made, as well as seeing whether you're keeping up with, or even surpassing, your original goals.

As I've mentioned, one of the top reasons why businesses fail is due to a lack of planning. Writing a detailed business plan that is geared toward the newsletter you want to publish will let you see if your goals fit in with your budget, if you should wait until you've raised more money, or indeed, if this is the right business for you after all.

Anyone who reads your business plan will be able to get a clear picture of the type of newsletter you want to publish, as well as its projected financial health. Spend the time on it now—if you run into trouble later on and don't have a business plan to refer back to, it just might be too late.

## Sample Business Plan

A business plan can be only a few pages long, or a massive 100-page document that maps out every single detail involved in publishing your newsletter.

Though it takes more time, it's best to err on the side of quantity when writing a business plan for your newsletter. The more you know about your business before you publish your first newsletter, the better prepared you will be for the surprises that may come your way.

A business plan should have five sections: A cover sheet, your statement of purpose for the newsletter, and a table of contents. Then, the meaty part: Section One describes the business: What you provide, your target markets, your location, competition, and personnel you expect to hire. Section Two concerns financial information about the newsletter: Income and cash flow projections, and if you're buying a newsletter from another owner, the financial history of the business as they ran it.

The last portion of your business plan should consist of supporting documents that back up the information you're providing in the other sections. A résumé of your employment history, your credit report, letters of reference, and any other items you believe will help the reader to better grasp what you are striving to do with your newsletter.

For an example of a sample business plan for a newsletter publishing business, see Appendix A, on page 193.

## Writing Your Marketing Plan

Though you do cover marketing to some extent in your business plan, developing and writing a separate, detailed marketing plan will serve the same clarifying purpose to your marketing efforts as to the development and daily operations of your newsletter.

Though you do have a lot of ideas to choose from in Chapter 7, without a concrete plan to follow, it's easy to let marketing fall to the bottom of your daily and weekly to-do lists, or even forget about it entirely.

Like in the business plan, in your marketing plan you'll define your pupose as well as the target audience you wish to reach with the various tools in your marketing arsenal. You'll design a marketing budget that is reasonable and aggressive at the same time, pick your choice of media, along with the methods you'll use to evaluate their results. This will help you to alter your marketing plan for the following year.

Marketing is usually considered to be an afterthought, something that is to be performed grudgingly when an advertising deadline looms or after you attend a trade association meeting and decide that your brochure and other promotional materials look painfully out of date compared to everyone else's.

One way to make marketing your business tolerable and even sometimes enjoyable is to map out a specific plan each year that won't let you off the hook so easily. If you say that in March it's time to send out your new brochure and guest newsletter, and that your budget that month allows for it, you'll do it.

The primary mistake that newsletter publishers make in their marketing is to rely too heavily on advertising, both when they're first starting out and later on as well. I'm not saying that advertising doesn't work, because in some cases it can pull quite well. However, it often turns out to be the most expensive way to reach customers, especially when your one-inch display ad is only one of hundreds in a particular publication.

Advertising is easy, and also a known entity with a tangible product—but it doesn't necessarily produce the results you desire, which is an increase in the number of customers. Advertising is easy because you tell the sales rep what you want to say, you write out a check, go over the proof, and receive a copy of the magazine. In other words, somebody else does all the work. Spending your time and money on promotion— whether it's sending out a press kit or renting a booth at a trade show—is harder, and doesn't provide you with a guaranteed entity, i.e., an ad in print. What it will do is provide you with increased exposure among your targeted customers;

they'll notice you simply because you'll stand out. After all, the majority of businesses take the easy way out, spending the bulk of their annual marketing budget on advertising and perhaps printing another 1,000 copies of their brochure with what's left over.

Developing a plan will help you to take a long-range view to spread your efforts among a variety of marketing opportunities. It will also help you to anticipate certain events that only happen once a year. But the plan is also meant to be tinkered with. For example, if a specific advertising issue comes up in September, or you hear about an idea that has worked wonders for another similar business nearby and you want to try it, you look at November and December and see you don't have much scheduled, even though your monthly marketing budget allows for $100. So you take the money from those two months and are able to pay for the project.

There are four different aspects to a marketing plan. They are:

1. The amount of time you will spend, on both a daily and weekly basis.

2. The type of marketing you plan to do, from concentrating on magazine publicity, newspaper ads, or revamping your brochure and business cards.

3. The amount of money you want to budget for each month and for the total year.

4. Who's going to carry out each task—for some businesses, only one person will be responsible for writing copy, working with a graphic artist, and doing interviews with the press. Even for the smallest businesses, some business owners decide to spread out the responsibilities to ensure they get done, and to provide a fresh eye.

The type of customer you're targeting enters into each of these aspects, broken down by region, profession, sex, income, and interests.

To draw up your annual marketing plan, you'll have to answer a lot of questions. You'll need to be as complete as possible, however, to design the best marketing plan for your business. Figure 4.2, Market Planning Assessment, on pages 79–80, helps to identify the questions that need answering.

---

*Advertising:* Radio, newspaper, TV, magazines, and directories of various trade associations.

*Direct Mail:* Sending brochures to prospective and past customers, sending information to magazines that deal with your specific topic.

*Publicity:* Sending letters, press releases and kits, and making followup calls.

---

To give you an idea of what a typical annual marketing plan for a newsletter looks like, see Appendix B, on page 205.

## Starting a Newsletter from Scratch

If you decide to start your newsletter from scratch, you will need to do more work from the beginning than if you bought an existing newsletter. The advantage of starting your own newsletter is that it costs less; it will also bear your personal stamp from the outset. Buying someone else's publication means that you'll have to work within a format and style that may not fit your own. You'll have to tinker with the formula slowly—even then, you may lose subscribers. Another disadvantage to starting your own is that it will take more time

**Figure 4.2:**

## Market Planning Assessment

### TIME

- How much time do you spend each week on marketing?

- Provide a breakdown of how many hours you'll spend each week on publicity, advertising, direct mail, and other areas. Do you feel this is enough time? Do you think you're using your time effectively?

- Would you like to spend more or less time? What would you spend it on, or where would you cut back?

- When do you project your busiest seasons to be? How far in advance should you begin planning for the various media and projects that you want to do?

- After you complete your first year in business, look back over the last calendar year. Which months were slow in terms of business? Which were busy?

### MEDIA

- In which media would you like to focus more of your marketing efforts?

- What type of marketing brings you the most customers?

- What kind of customer would you like to see more of? How would you reach them?

### BUDGET

- What percentage of total sales does your marketing budget comprise? How could you increase—or decrease—that amount? What other categories could you take money from?

- Do you have an annual or a monthly marketing budget now?

- Would you like to invest more money in one or more categories? Which ones? Why?

---

**Figure 4.2 (*cont.*)**

### EXECUTION

• Name the person or people currently responsible for marketing. Is there anyone else you feel comfortable assigning additional duties?

• Are there additional tasks you could assign to a staff member that you don't like to do or don't have enough time for?

### CUSTOMERS

• In which area of the country do most of your subscribers live? Are they concentrated in one industry, or is their profession not a consideration to the topic of your newsletter?

• What type of subscriber would you like to attract more of? How can you target them? Why would they be attracted to your newsletter?

Think about your answers to these questions for a few days. Is there anything missing?

---

before the money starts to come in steadily. You will also need to work hard on developing and building your reputation.

There's also a lot more detail and legal work to do if you start from scratch, which includes getting a business license, and setting yourself up as a business, all of which is covered in Chapter 5.

The main disadvantage to starting a newsletter from scratch is that you won't have income from the business until you start publishing the newsletter, which usually always takes longer than your initial estimates. In fact, while you do pay more at the outset for an existing newsletter, the business can start producing revenue for you from the day you move in. As you assume ownership, you also control the bank account and any subscriptions that come in after the transfer of ownership. You should weigh the pros and cons against your own temperament before you proceed. However, I find that the vast majority of newsletter publishers start their own newsletter because they have a burning desire to communicate about their topic.

If you buy an existing newsletter, most of the business technicalities have already been set up for you, from registering your business name to handling insurance for your business—though you do have to change everything over into your name.

You also have the advantage of having a track record that you can compare your own efforts to, though you still need to write a business and marketing plan.

Buying an established newsletter means that you have the advantage of a good reputation, and a well-developed list of subscribers who are loyal to your newsletter. Sometimes, buying an existing newsletter will actually cost less than starting from scratch if you factor in the reputation of the publication, the subscriber list, computer equipment, and other amenities that are included in the purchase price. And if you figure that your labor is worth something, even though you probably won't be paying yourself a salary for quite some time, buying a newsletter outright may turn out to be a veritable bargain.

I once sold a newsletter to the company that was handling my circulation duties. When the owner's lawyer sent me the first contract to arrange the sale, there was a clause that stated that after the sale transpired, I would be responsible for refunding the money to any subscriber who canceled their subscription. My lawyer struck the clause from the contract, and the buyer accepted it without a whimper. It's a good thing that we did remove the clause, because after the buyer took it over, they completely changed the direction of the newsletter and ended up folding it after only two issues under the new ownership.

## Action Guidelines

✔ Plan to start slowly when you start to publish your newsletter, and build gradually from there.

✔ Describe and visualize your newsletter down to the smallest detail.

✔ Write your business plan for your newsletter.

✔ Write your newsletter marketing plan.

✔ Determine whether buying an existing newsletter or starting from scratch would make the most sense for you.

$$\overset{\displaystyle Newsletter\ Publisher}{Profile}$$

## Cindy Larson
### *The CopyWriter* and *Just Copy*

It took a good number of years in academia before Cindy Larson discovered that she was doing the wrong thing. She was teaching American Literature at Boston University when she realized she hated what she was doing. "I was mad, because I had spent all this time pursuing this particular career and later found out that I had put the ladder up against the wrong wall," she said.

The turning point for her came in the fall of 1993 when she was offered a contract to teach for another two years at the school. She turned it down without knowing what she was going to do next, other than that it would involve writing and that she would work out of her home. And she sensed that even though she wasn't cut out for teaching, she knew she wanted to stay involved in the capacity of helping people learn.

She also read a lot of books about career changes and business magazines. What struck her in these publications was the ideas about career and change that the experts were coming up with were largely inaccessible to laypeople for two reasons. One, because most people simply didn't have the time to read, and two, many of these books that had the important new ideas were incredibly complex. Even if people did have the time and interest in these books, most would never pick them up because of their complexity.

After examining the possibilities, Larson started her company Narrative Strategies and began to publish a quarterly newsletter called, *The CopyWriter,* which was filled with articles that condensed the ideas from these leading business books into articles that were user-friendly. Her audience? Other newsletter editors, who would take these articles and use them in their own publications. Most of these editors are responsible for corporate newsletters that are distributed in-house to employees and also to present and prospective clients.

When she first thought up the idea, she called companies in the Boston area to talk to their newsletter editors. "We concentrated on talking with people in human resources, public relations, and training and development departments, since these people tended to have the job of producing the newsletter," says Larson. "We talked with them to find out what they were interested in, in terms of specific topics and article lengths, and then tried to write and design a newsletter that contained the information that they were looking for." For example, each article contains suggestions on how to slant the article as well as reducing the length for space considerations.

She then rented mailing lists of human resource employees in large and small companies, and took out small classified ads to attract editors who would pay $98 for a subscription to *The CopyWriter*. After *The CopyWriter* took off, Larson started a spinoff newsletter—*Just Copy*—also a quarterly, but half the size with shorter articles for newsletter editors at smaller companies who didn't have as much money to spend or didn't need the wide variety of articles presented in *The CopyWriter*. She also started a two-page newsletter called, *The Sampler,* so prospective subscribers could see if a subscription to one of the other newsletters would work for them. Larson offers them the free use of one article as a way for them so see if a subscription would work for them.

Larson writes most of the articles and reads most of the books the stories are based on while her partner, Dane Morrison—who is happy in his academic specialty of colonial business history—helps out with business angles and ideas. Most book publishers send free review copies to Larson, and she includes the title, author and publisher in each article that she bases on a particular book.

Since she began publishing newsletters in November, 1993, Larson has been approached by some people—mostly from trade and professional groups—who want to start publishing newsletters of their own. She's mulling this over, since she currently lacks the time to consult with others, but her advice falls on the conservative side: "If you have about a year's salary saved up, or can keep your current job, then go ahead and do it," she says. "You should keep in mind that it always takes a lot longer to start a new business than you think it will, and that goes for newsletters, too. It takes time to build up a subscription list, and I don't think a lot of people know that."

She also recommends that beginning newsletter publishers should talk with several publishing professionals in order to anticipate what some of their problems may be ahead of time. "If I had it to do over again, I'd use more professionals, like a graphic designer and an advertising and marketing expert," she says. "As it turned out, I did it all on my own and I did learn a lot, but I made some mistakes that could have been prevented."

An example she gives concerns direct mail packages. "Lots of newsletters are marketed through direct mail, and you really have to stand out. After all, there are a lot of design decisions you have to make when you only have a few seconds to catch somebody's eye, and a good design professional can help with that."

"It's also important that you also treat your newsletter like a business by staying close to your subscribers," she adds. "Get on the phone every so often and talk to your subscribers and ask what they want to see in the publication. A lot of the ideas in my newsletter are very much driven by what I hear from our subscribers. It's better than being the isolated expert or relying on other experts for your material."

Chapter
5

# GETTING STARTED

E very one of the details and aspects that are involved in publishing a newsletter will probably serve as the proving ground of your newsletter publishing business. After all, if you're still enthusiastic about publishing a newsletter after you've gotten through all the grunt work that's necessary to get your first issue written, edited, and published, then you know you've made the right decision.

Even if you've fallen slightly out of love with your newsletter after the start-up tasks, you shouldn't worry, because the moment you receive your first subscription check in the mail or your first congratulatory letter to the editor, all the reasons why you wanted to start publishing a newsletter will come rushing back at you.

You just have to jump through a few hoops first.

## How to Test Your Newsletter Idea

The first thing you should do is to check out the competition. Indeed, you need to find out if any competition does exist and if you think that your newsletter will be different enough that you will be able to attract subscribers and even pull some of the subscribers away from your competition.

Check out a copy of one of several newsletter directories out there. (See Chapter 3 for a list.) Your library may have one of them. Look under the subject indexes and analyze the titles of publications that exist. Is the one you're thinking of already taken? Or is there one that is particularly clever that inspires you to change your title?

If you find any competitors listed, jot down the address, and send for a sample copy. Or better yet, call and say that you'd like to subscribe and that you'd like some information. The direct mail piece that the newsletter sends to you will reveal a lot about the newsletter, and more so, the type of reader they're trying to attract. Order a sample issue. Then, if they accept advertising— either classified or display ads—ask them to send you their ad rate sheet. You'll see how much they charge for ads, circulation figures, and a breakdown of their subscription base, if the newsletter has conducted a readership survey.

Analyze the articles, the tables of contents of back issues of the newsletter—if they are listed—and the tone of the editorial. How different is your image of your newsletter? How can you improve on what this publication is doing? Can you broaden or narrow your topic in order to attract a subscriber to your newsletter, as well as others who have already made the decision not to subscribe to your potential competition?

If you have not located a competitor, keep in mind that there are thousands of newsletters that aren't listed in the newsletter directories, either because the directory publishers didn't know about them or else the newsletter editor declined to be listed in the directory. At this point, your goal is to start snooping around. Also at your library, you'll find the massive three-volume *Encyclopedia of Associations*, which lists thousands of associations and social groups all over the country, some for topics that are so esoteric that you would never imagine that a group existed to study the topic and service people who are interested in it.

The *Encyclopedia* is organized by subject, so it will be easy for you to research the groups. Your work at this point is twofold. One, to research the groups that may publish a newsletter on your topic, and two, to take note of the groups that will be interested in hearing about your newsletter when you publish your first issue. Since many of the associations listed in the *Encyclopedia* publish newsletters for their members only, I wouldn't really consider these publications to be your competition, because you'll be striving for a larger audience. But again, as with the other subscription newsletters you've researched, send for information on each similar organization as well as a sample copy of their newsletter. Remember to compare the content of each publication with the vision you have for yours.

The next step is to call some experts in your field to test the validity of your subject, and also that you've targeted it accurately enough. For instance, returning to the example of the menu newsletter for working mothers, call up a nutritionist in your area, or better yet, at your nearest university or college. Say that you're calling from your publishing company and that you're test-marketing an idea for a newsletter and want to get her professional opinion. Some questions you'll want to ask include:

- What do you think of the idea of this newsletter?
- Has anything similar recently come across your desk?
- What types of topics would you like to see covered in such a publication?

- Can you recommend a particular group, book, or resource I can turn to for more information?
- Is there anything else you'd like to tell me about the topic?
- Is there anyone else you think could provide me with feedback on this topic?

Then thank her for her time, promise her a copy of your first issue, and lastly dangle the possibility of a position on your advisory board.

Whenever I start to think about publishing a new newsletter, I try to talk to at least ten people in that particular field before I proceed, even if I know I'm going ahead with it anyway. This early respect and feedback will help you go a long way toward shaping not only your first issue but issues to come.

## Naming Your Business

If you want to publish a newsletter, you'll have to come up with two different names. One, obviously, is for your newsletter. While you're at it, you should also pick another, different name for your business.

Why two names? Some newsletter publishers run their publishing companies as one entity. To them, the name of their newsletter *is* the name of their business. But to me this is extremely short-sighted, since you'll probably want to expand your business somewhere down the road, which may include publishing additional newsletters, directories, and books, as well as producing seminars, trade shows, and other events. So as long as you believe the sky's the limit as far as your business is concerned, and that the newsletter you're thinking of publishing now is just the beginning, you should pick a relatively nondescript name for your business that is able to encompass all future projects as well as convey a professional image to subscribers and customers.

Many people name their publishing businesses after themselves. This works if you're a consulting firm, but not if you're a one-person business just starting out where you're the only one who answers your business phone line. Some use their initials—as in LAN Publications—but again, I don't feel that this says anything.

Pick a name that is amorphous, a name that means something personally to you, and that sends a certain professional message about your business. I'll use my own business—Williams Hill Publishing—as an example.

When I started publishing *Sticks*, my fourth newsletter, in the spring of 1994, I needed to find a company name. In the past, I've looked to local geographical maps as well as other local businesses for ideas. In my area, there are at least five businesses named after Moose Mountain, a geographical landmark that is located a few towns away from me. That sounded good as a company name for *Sticks*, I surmised, and so I decided that it would serve as my business name. I also knew I would be starting up another newsletter two months later, so the title seemed to be a good fit.

Until I went to register my business name with the state, that is, which promptly informed me that the name was already taken. (Of course, I had already bull-headedly ignored all the advice in every single business book that told me to register a business name with the state before printing up stationery, checks, etc. My bank was very trusting; they assumed that I had already done my homework and never asked to see my business certificate. But when I went back to change the name several months later, they *did* ask to see it.) Although it was a bit of a pain, part of me was glad I had to change it, since to me and my associates' ears, Moose Mountain did sound a bit hickish, not an image I wanted my business to portray over the long haul.

The second time out, I got out the local maps again. I rejected Half-Moon Press after a local pond (some might say it sounded half-baked), Grafton Press (I might move), and Cardigan Mountain Publishing (too close to another publisher, Cadogan Guides). A nearby road caught my eye—actually a road I planned to buy land on—and Williams Hill Publishing was born. I chose *Publishing* instead of *Press* because *Press* sounds like it limits itself to printed matter, and I knew I wanted to pursue publishing databases on computer disk. The name was suitably professional, I had a personal connection to it, and both *Sticks* and *Travel Marketing Bulletin* fit well into it.

On to naming your newsletter. Please, nothing with *Spectrum, Image, Notes,* or *News* in the title. They're used too much now as it is, and they don't really say anything. *Sticks* just popped into my head one morning while I was making my list of 100 article ideas, but *Travel Marketing Bulletin* was more specifically crafted.

There was already a newsletter with the name *Travelwriter Marketletter,* and another by the name of *Inn Marketing.* According to my spies, a newsletter by the name of *Successful Hotel Marketer* was about to go belly up, which would be useful later on when I was scouting for writers.

My newsletter would show inns, B&Bs, outfitters, travel bureaus, and other small travel businesses how to market themselves better with lots of case histories, tips, and ideas. I basically knew I wanted to use *Travel* and *Marketing,* but I wasn't sure about anything else. I looked at other newsletters, some of which used *News* and *Notes,* both of which I hated. I typed them into the computer anyway, and used the thesaurus function. *Bulletin* popped out at me. For another newsletter I plan to publish, the subject is how to run your business better. The main word will be *Business.*

If you're stuck, go back to one of the newsletter directories and flip through the listings for newsletters whose topics have nothing to do with yours. Remember, the title of your newsletter doesn't have to be fancy, but it should give a hint of what the publication is about.

Whether your title is clear or not—*Travel Marketing Bulletin* in the first instance, *Sticks* in the second—it's a good idea to have a subtitle that clearly spells out your focus and to use it as your subtitle as well as referring to it in your marketing materials. For *Sticks*, it's "for people who want to move to the country;" *Travel Marketing Bulletin*'s is "helping small travel businesses market themselves more effectively."

What does your newsletter help readers to know? In a brief phrase, use it as your subtitle.

## Your Newsletter and the Law

With any business, there are certain legal restrictions that you have to meet in order to do business. The good news is that with a newsletter publishing business, the law has minimal impact in terms of getting your business off the ground.

The first thing you need to do is register your business with the state. There will be a fee for this, and the purpose is to make sure no other business is currently operating with your name. If there is, you will have to find another name for your business. You may also want to register the name of your newsletter with the state, although I've found it to be unnecessary.

Registration will also alert the state to expect tax revenue from your business. If you don't file a return with the state, they'll know where to find you.

When you register with the state, you should also ask about other regulations you have to meet in order to operate as a publishing company in your state. Most of the time, they will refer you to your town, which is responsible for determining zoning and other business regulations, since it will collect the fees from any permits for renovations that you will need to make.

I will get into the nitty gritty of the various bureaucracies later in this chapter. The important things at this point is to find out what departments the state, town, or county are each responsible for, the type of registration you will have to make with each, and to make sure you comply with all of them. If you neglect any one of the steps necessary to open and operate a newsletter publishing company in your town, the government authorities at any level have the power to shut down your business and/or do whatever is necessary in order to bring your business into compliance. The time to find all of this out is before you open your doors. It pays to do your homework first.

You'll also need to determine the form of business you'll run: a sole proprietorship, partnership, or a corporation. Each has its advantages and disadvantages, and newsletter publishers have very specific reasons for picking one over the others.

## Sole Proprietorship

A sole proprietorship is the form of business that most single-owner businesses pick. It's easy to start—all you have to do is register with the state and you're in business. You make all the decisions yourself, and except for zoning concerns regarding running your business from your home, you're pretty much free from having to follow complex laws regarding the operation of your business. You alone are responsible for the success or failure of your business, and any profits that your newsletter earns are reported as income in your name.

However, because there are few restrictions on a sole proprietorship when you run into legal or financial trouble, it falls on your shoulders to deal with it. For many newsletter publishers, liability insurance that's tied in with your business or homeowners policy will often be enough to handle a "reasonable" lawsuit and settlement. The remote chances of being hit with a lawsuit and the relative ease of operating this form of business ownership make a sole proprietorship the preferred method of business organization for most newsletter publishers.

However, if your business should fail, you will be responsible for all outstanding debts incurred during the course of doing business. If you don't pay them, or declare bankruptcy, it will be reflected on your personal credit record.

## Partnerships

A partnership is actually two sole proprietorships combined. This means that while the strengths are doubled, so are the inherent weaknesses.

The most common instance where a newsletter publisher decides to create a partnership is choosing to enter the business with a friend or business partner. Married couples also sometimes decide to form a partnership when the begin to publish a newsletter together. Though a partnership usually means that twice as much energy and money are available than in a sole proprietorship, you should consider it very carefully before you proceed. The best partnerships work when the partners have differing but complementary talents—and they leave the other partner alone to do what they do best. For instance, at one newsletter, one partner may have a strong background in marketing and day-to-day business operations, while the other loves nothing more than to write, research, and edit the newsletter. As long as each trusts the other to concentrate on their own department, and to interfere only when problems arise, then the partnership will probably do well.

Partnerships usually run into trouble when the partners have similar skills and/or different ideas about the right way to run a business. For example, when both partners want to concentrate on writing the newsletter, but not deal with the behind-the-scenes tasks of entering new subscriptions into the computer database or work with the printer, there are going to be problems right from the start.

As with a sole proprietorship, if somebody decides to sue the newsletter, usually for libel or remarks that the subject perceives as anti-inflammatory, both partners are personally liable. And if the business fails leaving outstanding debts, again, you are both responsible. You should also be aware that if one partner disappears after a newsletter fails, the other must pay all debts. Be aware of this, because this does happen from time to time.

## Corporations

A corporation is best defined as an inanimate object, a business organization that has its own needs aside from those of the business, which include financial and legal restrictions. It's more difficult, expensive, and time-consuming to form and then operate your newsletter as a corporation, but it also absolves your formal personal responsibility in case business sours or a customer or in the rare case that someone decides to sue.

One advantage that corporations have over partnerships or sole proprietorships is that this form of business can raise money by selling shares in the business; the only recourse the other two have is to borrow money from a bank or from friends.

A corporation is by nature more unwieldy than the other two because of its responsibility to its shareholders, who are really part-owners. The IRS taxes corporations on a different scale from sole proprietorships and partnerships, and there are even more rules and regulations a corporation must follow on both the state and federal level. There are also certain restrictions on the types of operations a corporation can run—some expansion and growth issues, for example, require the approval of stockholders before a project can proceed.

Some newsletter publishers automatically opt for incorporation to protect their personal assets in the case of a lawsuit, and this is prudent. However, a newsletter business that will benefit most from incorporation is when there are more than two owners controlling the future of the business. With multiple partners deciding the fate of the newsletter, issues of ownership, and decision-making necessarily become more complex, so it becomes easier to rely on a board of directors and group of stockholders, especially since they've invested their money and trust in the business.

## Do You Need an Attorney?

Whether or not you choose to use the services of an attorney to help you set up your newsletter publishing company before you publish your first issue depends on how you view the legal profession in addition to how detail-oriented you are. Some newsletter publishers swear by their lawyers and consult with them about every decision that needs to be made. Others swear *at* them, and will never use an attorney for anything in their business or personal lives.

The happy medium is somewhere in between. If you're planning to incorporate your newsletter publishing business, you'll probably need to use a lawyer, although more people are learning how to incorporate themselves. I feel that the vast majority use a lawyer to help facilitate the process.

If, however, you're buying an established newsletter, you will undoubtedly have to hire an attorney to negotiate the terms of the contract. Aside from this, you will probably be able to do most of the tasks involved in starting your newsletter without a lawyer.

## Do You Need an Accountant?

If you're unsure about the type of business organization that suits you best—sole proprietorship, partnership, or corporation—it's a good idea to consult with an accountant to help you decide. An accountant will analyze your current financial situation and help you determine what you want to gain from publishing a newsletter in terms of revenue—equity or income—and advise you about how to best achieve your goals.

An accountant can also analyze the books and financial records of a newsletter that you're thinking about buying. It's a good idea to find an accountant who has some experience keeping the books for small publishing companies; you may want to ask other newsletter publishers in your area for the names of some accountants they'd recommend to you. Then call each of them up and interview them before you settle on one.

An accountant can also help you set up a realistic budget and a schedule of projected revenues. If this is the first time you've run a business of your own, a professional accountant can help you become familiar with different accounting methods, the tax rates based on projected revenue, and the tax codes of your state. An accountant can also recommend methods of bookkeeping that will make their job that much easier when tax season rolls around.

## Licenses and Permits

Before you print the first issue of your newsletter, you must check with the local, county, and state business authorities to find out about the various kinds of licenses and permits you'll need in order to be licensed, if any. Also, if you're running your business out of your home, you should check with your local town ordinances to see the kinds of restrictions—if any—that are placed on home-based businesses. All of these vary from town to town and from state to state, so I'm not going to go into detail about them here.

I will, however, describe the purpose of the licenses and permits you will be required to get. Bear in mind, however, the stringency of these requirements will also vary as well. States and regions with more highly regulated governments tend to be pickier about what you can and cannot do with your business, and the fees they charge you for the privilege of making enough money to pay taxes.

Even though you may resent all the legalese and paper-work, it's important to meet all of the requirements. No one says you can't complain every step of the way, however. You'll need a sales tax certificate from the state to collect tax on any in-state mail-order purchases your subscribers will make from you. A health inspector may need to ascertain whether your septic and water systems can accommodate the increased demands that employees and visitors will place on them.

Even if your home and facilities successfully meet all of the above regulations, if your home is not in an area that is zoned for business use, you may be out of luck and will need to run your business from an office in an area that's especially zoned for commercial use. However, it's your town government that determines zoning and is also responsible for making exceptions for publishing companies and other small businesses that are located outside of commercial zones. Though your business will provide a tax base for your town and help bring more money to local businesses that you will frequent, since you will have a commercial enterprise operating in a residential area, you will probably have to apply for a zoning variance.

The rules get creative, though. Some towns will allow you to operate your business at home as long as you don't hang out a sign. Others will require that you as owner live in the house and not in a separate building. You may also have to expand your driveway and parking area to accommodate an increased number of cars.

And far more interesting laws governing small businesses in your area undoubtedly exist. That's why it's important to check all of the requirements *before* you do anything.

## Action Guidelines

✔ Pick a name for your newsletter as well as for your publishing company.

✔ Determine what form of business you'd like—sole proprietorship, partnership, or corporation.

✔ Find out about the legal requirements you'll have to meet, from license and permits to zoning exemptions.

## Newsletter Publisher Profile

### Gil Gordon
### *Telecommuting Review*

Gil Gordon has always been a little ahead of his time, which is a good trait to have if you're going to publish a newsletter.

In the early 80s, Gordon was starting his consulting business in the field of telecommuting. Even though the field was basically in its infancy back then, he developed a steady roster of clients and kept busy with his work. In 1984, a colleague suggested that Gordon begin publishing a newsletter on the burgeoning industry—at the time there was no publication on the subject—and after some consideration, he published the first issue in October, 1984. But first, he wanted to test the waters.

"I sent a direct mail package for the newsletter to my mailing list, and our goal was that if we received 50 subscriptions from that first mailing that we would go ahead with it," says Gordon. Sixty people responded, and these people who received the first issue were very enthusiastic about it.

"In retrospect, I don't know what possessed me to do these things, since I never saw myself as being in the newsletter business," he says. "I always viewed the newsletter as an adjunct to my consulting business, since consulting sold more newsletter subscriptions than the other way around." But he saw that once he began publishing the newsletter he became an instant authority. He was also the first one out of the gates to publish a newsletter on the subject. "Longevity is worth something," he adds.

Since he began publishing *Telecommuting Review*, he has written about 90 percent of the articles that appear in the monthly publication, which averages 12 to 14 pages an issue. He says that he's going to solicit more outside writers to contribute to the newsletter, but that there is a dilemma in doing so. "I'm finding that one of the things people like in the newsletter is my individual insight and comments, which I discovered as the result of a reader survey," he says. "Since then, I've been changing the articles to reflect an increase in analysis and less straight news, but with getting outside writers I have to be prepared to editorialize their articles, or change the focus. It's a precarious balance." He adds the hardest thing about writing the newsletter is incorporating this analysis into each article. "It's taking material that's newsworthy and going a level above reporting what happened by trying to share information that really adds knowledge to what's going on out there. It's really the difference between a news story and an op-ed piece."

Gordon says writing the newsletter takes about two or three days a month. Then, instead of producing it himself, he sends the copy to a publisher in California who handles the production, layout, and mailing for a fee.

His circulation consists of several hundred readers who are primarily corporate human resource staff, managers in telecommunications departments, managers in corporate

departments where there are telecommuters, as well as vendors who want to see what's going on in the marketplace and what it says about how they're marketing their product.

In order to expand to larger markets, Gordon started a conference on telecommuting in 1992 and found it was so successful that he expanded it and began holding it as an annual event. "Again, it was a case of the one who was there first having the advantage," he said. "Even though we had no idea what we were doing and I thought we were going to lose our shirts, we ended up making some money." An interesting fact is that many of the 101 people who attended the conference that first year had been approached by Gordon about his consulting services, but he never worked with them. "I'm beginning to see that there are different customers who prefer their information in a variety of forms. Some will buy consulting, others will buy the newsletter, a videotape, book, or conference," he says.

He's attracted most of the subscribers to his newsletter through publicity and word of mouth, but is expanding into doing more direct mail. He suggests that beginning newsletter publishers find their niche, stick with it, and do the best job they can. And since he is deeply involved in the electronic age, he makes the following point: "You could argue that a print product like a newsletter doesn't make sense anymore. In fact, I have that argument a lot of time with myself. I do list the newsletter on a couple of databases right now, but I still think that something like this requires some effort to read, since it's not a quick read. There's also a fair amount of pass-along readership with my newsletter. There's something that's tangible about paper that makes it easy to pass it along that's not there with a computer screen."

# OPERATING YOUR NEWSLETTER

O perations—the day-to-day routine you set up and follow in order to maintain some semblance of organization to help you publish your newsletter— is not the most fun or creative part of your business, like meeting with some of the top experts in your field or being interviewed by the press. In fact, I'll be the first to admit it: operations can be downright boring.

But neglecting these steps and running your daily operations in a haphazard way is the quickest way to drive your business right into the ground. Take some time now to set daily operations policy; later on, it will mean that you'll have more time for the fun stuff.

## Estimating Operating Costs

Every business has its cycles when business is booming and then when it stops dead in its tracks. Unfortunately, there are a certain number of bills and business expenses that continue to accrue unfettered; they don't care that you haven't gotten in any new subscriptions in the last week. They still demand to be paid.

Publishing a newsletter is no exception. In my experience, it will take about six months of constant marketing and promotion before you can expect to see steady revenue flowing into your business. As you'll see in Chapter 7, it takes that long for your product to register in the minds of prospective customers. And as I've also said, some people will need to hear about your newsletter and the idea of subscribing several times before they even think about responding to your subscription offer. So consider yourself to be forewarned.

There are also several times during the year that are notorious for stopping the flow of new subscriptions and renewals dead in their tracks. One is the summertime. Especially for a newsletter that promises to help the reader improve themselves in some way, either in their personal life or at work, which is the thrust of the majority of newsletters that are published today. Summer is a time to lounge and enjoy life. December is another time of year when people are thinking of spending money on other people, and not necessarily on themselves. Again, the idea of enjoying themselves and putting off any self-improvement programs until after New Year's is the rule, rarely the exception. So be sure to put away some money ahead of time to get you through these slow times. Because your expenses will continue to accumulate without regard for your greatly reduced income.

If you are purchasing an established newsletter, estimating your operating costs will be easy. Just ask the current owners for a full year's breakdown of expenses along with the current income statement. If possible, go through the expenses with the owners asking about the budgeted amounts and the actual expenses. If you are starting from scratch, it will be a little more difficult to estimate your operating costs, but you can still give it a shot. Be aware, however, that most novice publishers greatly underestimate what every one of their expense categories will cost them. You may want to ask a newsletter publisher who you've become friendly with what he or she spends on printing and postage each month, as well as some of the highest expenses. Some people will think that you're being too nosy and will either give you inaccurate figures on purpose or else none at all. Regardless of this, the best way to estimate your operating costs is to contact the suppliers you'll be dealing with. They will probably be very helpful, especially if it looks like you'll be spending significant amounts of money with them in the future.

Figure 6.1 is a chart that contains all possible expenses you may encounter in publishing a newsletter. I won't provide estimates, since they can vary so widely depending on what your early goals are in terms of mailing solicitations to potential subscribers, how much promotion and marketing you plan to do, whether you will work at home or outside, whether you hire help, and so on. You can also use this chart to see which categories you can cut back on or even eliminate entirely. It's a good idea to chart the expenses for each month for a year—some are optional, and you may be able to cut down on some expenses you can do yourself.

Figure 6.1:

## Possible Newsletter Expenses

### Your Office

Note: For a home-based business, figure your business share of each type of expense, according to the percentage of space your office occupies in the house.

### Overhead

Mortgage/rent
Taxes
Insurance
Utilities
Heat

Figure 6.1 (*cont.*)

## Office Expenses

Telephone
Separate fax line
Credit card commissions
Postage
Stationery supplies
Printing
Advertising
  Mailing list rentals
  Mailing house services
Consultants
Miscellaneous marketing fees
Trade show booth rentals
Travel agency commissions
Trade association dues and memberships
Accountant and attorney fees
Contract employees, freelance writers, editors, and
  designers
Computer equipment
Software

## Company Vehicle

Loan
Registration
Insurance
Gas

## Employee Expenses

Payroll
Taxes
Insurance
Workers' compensation
Bonuses
Discounts

# Keeping Good Records

Once you get your newsletter up and running and published on a regular schedule, it's important to keep track of your expenses and revenue sources. On the one hand, it will make things easier for you at tax time, but it's also enlightening to know how much you spent by sorting your newsletter in-house and sending your newsletter out first-class last year, and to figure out how much money—and time—you could save at the end of the year by switching to bulk mail or an automated mailing service instead.

There are as many ways to keep records as there are newsletter publishers. Some rely on a standard spreadsheet computer program specially designed to help keep track of several different kinds of revenue and many different types of expenses. Some stuff receipts in shoe boxes and dump them out at the end of the year, leaving a large task for their accountant to handle.

No matter which method you choose, you should make it easy to do and organize it so you can do it immediately instead of saving up the work to be done in one unmanageable lump at the end of the week. If you're like most newsletter publishers, you'll discover that it will be difficult to find an uninterrupted block of time anywhere in your week unless it's in the wee hours of the morning.

In the unlikely case of a tax audit somewhere down the road, it will undoubtedly help boost your case if you can show the auditor receipts that provide answers to all questions. Keeping good records will also help facilitate figuring out the deductions you'll be able to take.

Keeping good records also helps you to determine the annual percentage of subscriptions that come in each month in order to help you track your peak and slow times, as well as knowing where each subscriber heard about you. This is important when you start to plan future marketing campaigns so you'll know which ad or promotion brought in the largest number of subscriptions. That way you can concentrate your marketing in the same places next year.

Keeping adequate records just makes good common sense. At the very least, you should get a ledger book to organize your records. Some business checking accounts now offer a shortcut in the form of built-in ledger that allows you to break down the checks you write into different expense categories thus eliminating the need for a separate ledger.

## Accounting Basics

Once you start publishing your newsletter, you need to keep track of revenue coming in and expenses going out. It's a good idea to set up an accounting system that works best for you and your business.

There are two kinds of accounting you can use to track revenue and expenses. One is cash accounting and it involves simple bookkeeping where income is recorded when it is received, and expenses that are paid are recorded when bills go out, even if the expense was incurred in a different month. For instance, say a subscriber buys $50 worth of Special Reports and books that you sell on the last day of a month. You deposit the check or charge the purchase to their credit card, the same day, but the income is not posted in your account until a few days later, which happens to fall in the next month. With cash accounting, you will record the revenue in the month where it may not have necessarily occurred. This may give you an inaccurate picture of your business cycles if you rely on revenue alone to show the health of your business, and not month-to-month subscriber rate. Cash accounting, however, is a very simple way to keep your books, and many newsletter publishers prefer it for its simplicity. They tend to be running a small one-person business that is not yet pulling in a significant amount of money; as a result, they don't need a precise picture of their month-to-month revenue and expense picture.

Accrual accounting is more painstaking in its execution, but it gives a more accurate view of revenue and expenses, and of your monthly financial situation. Even though payment may be received or credited the following month—and expenses paid on a net 30 system since the expenses occurred in the previous month—they are recorded in that month's ledgers, and not when they were actually paid.

When drawing up your accounting sheets, no matter which method you choose, refer to the categories named in the previous section, Estimating Operating Costs. You may want to list certain expenses in categories that are even more specific. Think carefully about the method and categories that will work best for your business.

## Your Daily Tasks

Managing a newsletter publishing business, like any small business, requires that you be a good juggler and able to switch back and forth between a variety of tasks. Publishing a newsletter is different from many other small businesses, however, since the tasks are so different and disparate. For instance, one minute you may be writing an article for the next issue of your newsletter, and a half hour later you may be working with your accountant, while 15 minutes later you may get a call from a subscriber who just wants to chat. If you are unable to switch gears quickly, you should think about putting somebody else in charge of certain tasks where you find it difficult to jump in head first.

The Typical Business Day described in Chapter 1 gives you a good idea of the variety of tasks you'll be called on to perform each day in the course of running your newsletter publishing business. Some of the duties, however, won't be necessary for you to handle each day; sometimes certain tasks get bunched up all on one day or during a certain period of the month or year. It's up to you to be prepared to handle them—or have someone else who is. And once you start publishing your newsletter on a regular basis, you'll be able to develop a feel for the rhythm of the business and actually be able to anticipate some of the necessary tasks before they reach the Immediate Attention Requested stage.

## Hiring Employees

Some newsletter publishers prefer to keep their operations as small, one-person businesses, specifically so they'll be able to handle all the jobs themselves without having to hire outside help. Hiring and managing employees adds a whole new dimension into your business and has both its good and bad points. For one, it means more paperwork because you'll have to pay state, federal, and perhaps local payroll taxes in addition to Social Security, workers' compensation, and insurance— that is, if you decide to offer it. On the other hand, having someone around to help out with the grunt work means you'll have more time to focus on running and building your business, like marketing your newsletter and exploring new ancillary products to sell to your growing subscriber base.

Unfortunately, a common complaint of business owners everywhere today is that it's hard to find good help; after all, no paid employee is going to regard your business and customers in the same meticulous and painstaking light that you will. So you'll probably have to lower your standards of quality and attention and plan to spend some time making up for the lack.

With the rise in unlawful sexual harassment suits brought as the result of being fired, many newsletter publishers have been further discouraged from hiring help, even though they may want to.

Many newsletter publishers advise that if you find an employee who is the exception to the rule, hold onto that person as tightly as you can by increasing his or her pay, offering bonuses, and letting this person know how much you appreciate him or her with added responsibilities and the occasional day off with pay.

When hiring employees, there are certain things you have to do. If you're hiring a person to work for you regularly, writing, answering the phone and/or stuffing envelopes, they will be considered to be your employee and you will have to deduct taxes from their paycheck, which you will have to file with the government either quarterly or once a year, depending on your tax setup.

Some businesses get around the process of withholding and payroll taxes by preferring to hire an employee as an independent contractor. This way, the contractor files a self-employment tax, which saves you a lot of paperwork. This works for such seasonal and periodic workers as gardeners and musicians, but it will send up red flags with the IRS if you try to hire a part-time office assistant in this way. If you do hire an independent contractor, and pay them more than $600 over the course of a year, you must file a 1099 form on their behalf which reports their income.

No matter how you decide to "hire" an employee, make sure that you always communicate with them clearly and directly and immediately when there's a problem or complaint. And let them know when you think they did a job well.

## Working with Suppliers

When you're first starting out, you'll probably buy your supplies—stationery, computer equipment, and office supplies—from stores and businesses you already have dealt with in the past. Later on, as you grow, you might want to deal directly with wholesalers, commercial distributors, mailing houses, and larger printers, but even if you do reach that point, you still might prefer to do it all yourself by working with a smaller printer who costs more but is a ten-minute drive away, or hiring a part-time assistant to help out with mailing crunches when an issue needs to be mailed out.

The first issue you'll face when approaching suppliers is that they usually require large minimum orders so that they can keep their costs down. For instance, instead of printing up 1,000 copies, the minimum print run is 5,000. Obviously, even if the per-copy cost is half the price, if you only need 1,000 copies, you'll lose money even if you sell back issues of your newsletter, since you're not going to be able to sell that many to account for the money you'll keep tied up in them. Not to mention the overhead that's necessary to store them. The surprise may come when you compare the prices of the larger printer with your small local printer: you may discover that the big company's prices are actually higher than your local printer, since they may include the cost of delivering the supplies to you in their overhead while they tell you that it's free. Even for a distributor who deals in more than one type of supplies, your combined potential order might be too small for the company to want to bother with you.

If you're like most newsletter publishers, in the beginning, anyway, you'll probably have to do everything yourself out of economic necessity, from shopping for stationery and office supplies and delivering camera-ready copy to the printer. Some local businesses will allow you to set up a house charge account to simplify your bookkeeping and so that you can send a staff or family member to the store to pick up a couple of boxes of envelopes, making it unnecessary to dig up some cash. Some of these "suppliers" will also offer you a discount for buying in quantity and also for paying before net 30 days.

Even if you do it all yourself, however, it still pays to shop around. When buying office supplies, for instance, you'll probably spend the most at your neighborhood stationery store. The next cheapest source will be a stationery superstore, though sometimes the quality and attention you'll receive is far below what you're used to. In my experience, the cheapest source of office supplies are the mail-order operations that ship the same day your order is received and offer large discounts on volume orders on top of their already low prices.

There are exceptions to everything, however, so the best advice is to take your time and shop around and don't be afraid to dicker. These companies want your business, and if you show you're going to be a good, steady customer, they'll work hard to keep you.

## Understanding Taxes

When you first set up your new publishing business and discover how much time, energy, and paperwork you devote to taxes, you might wonder when you'll find the time to write the articles and market your newsletter. Between payroll taxes and your own income and other personal taxes, it can all seem pretty self-defeating at this point. Why go into business if most of your revenue will go toward taxes?

First of all, take a deep breath. It only seems overwhelming now as you're learning about your different responsibilities. Once you get used to it, recording and paying taxes—as well as figuring out your deductions—will turn out to consume just a small part of your bookkeeping and office time. As I've mentioned earlier, this is why it's important to keep good records.

For one, you will also be required to keep track of your revenue and expenses and to pay a tax to the IRS on any profit your newsletter earns. The amount of tax you pay will depend on the type of business you're running: a sole proprietorship, partnership, or a corporation. The tax structures for each differ.

Of course, since the start-up costs for a newsletter publishing business are so high during the couple of years you're in business, your expenses may exceed your income, so you won't have to pay tax. The IRS allows that there will be years when you'll earn no profit on paper, even though it assumes you are in business to earn a profit. As a result, many businesses claim a wealth of deductions to avoid showing·a profit, and therefore, paying tax. That's why current tax law says that you must show a profit at least three years out of five to prove that you are running a viable business. If you show a loss three or more years out of the five, again, this will alert the IRS and set you up for the possibility of an audit. This is why some newsletter publishers, even though they may lose money on paper in a given year, may decide to "forget" about some deductions just to avoid arousing the suspicions of the IRS. Keep in mind that the deductions claimed by home businesses always come under more scrutiny from the IRS.

As for payroll taxes, contact your state employment bureau about the exact deductions you should make for each employee, in addition to the federal tax bureau for information about income tax, Social Security, and other payroll taxes.

## Action Guidelines

✔ Estimate in advance what it will cost to write, edit, print, and send out each issue of your newsletter.

✔ Develop a system that painlessly allows you to maintain accurate records.

✔ Set the subscription rates for your newsletters according to what other newsletters charge.

✔ Pick cash accounting or accrual accounting as a way to set up your books.

✔ Be clear about the pros and cons of hiring employees for your newsletter publishing business.

*Newsletter Publisher Profile*

### Elaine Floyd
*Newsletter News & Resources*

Elaine Floyd was one of the pioneers in the newsletter business back in the early 80s, except she was writing and editing non-subscription newsletters as a sales tool. She was working on the first Macintosh computer that came out using Page-Maker version 1.

Floyd's background was in engineering, and she was working in sales and marketing for a high-tech company in Nashville. "I was driving all over the south, and I was so busy that I frequently forgot to tell my clients everything they needed to know," she said. So she started publishing a newsletter that provided her clients with the information she might have left out of her meetings. When her company saw how well the newsletter worked to increase sales in Floyd's territory, they decided they wanted to distribute it company-wide and use it as a marketing tool for a dozen salespeople. Floyd was sending her newsletter to the company's art department, who took care of laying it out and typesetting it. However, Floyd saw she could buy a Macintosh of her own with the money the company was spending on designing just one issue, so the company assigned her the responsibility for the newsletter. Once she had the equipment, however, she began to look for other newsletter jobs in her moonlighting hours. Soon, she had a full-fledged business going, and she decided to get out of travel and sales.

Soon, she was producing newsletters for 25 clients from mostly high-tech and industrial companies with four full-time employees. However, she found that she was spending more time managing her employees and business and less working on the newsletter, which is what she preferred. When a chance came to move to New Orleans for her husband's promotion, she took it, disbanded the business, and set out to start from scratch again.

She again started producing newsletters for corporate clients, but was determined to keep her business small the second time around. In order to promote her business, she designed a promotional newsletter to tout her services. She received some jobs, yes, but more importantly, she heard from people who wanted to subscribe to her promotional newsletter. After some hesitation, she began to convert her newsletter into what has grown into *Newsletter News & Resources*, a quarterly 8-page publication for newsletter writers and designers and entrepreneurs who are producing their own newsletters and need some guidance in doing it.

Floyd says that the biggest difference between producing a client newsletter and a subscription newsletter is knowing that people are paying for the information she is publishing. "I have so much pressure on me to publish information that's valuable and fresh that it takes me so much longer to do my own newsletter than if it was strictly a marketing piece," she says.

Though she charges $19.95 for a subscription, she still uses the newsletter as a promotional piece for her other products, which have grown to include several books on how to publish a newsletter to promote your own business or somebody else's, and how to use the newsletter to market your business. Her first book, *Marketing with Newsletters*, has sold 13,000 copies through lectures, seminars, bookstores, and mail order. She also thinks about forming a newsletter society where subscribers would purchase a membership and be entitled to a subscription to *Newsletter News & Resources*, a book or two, a directory of newsletter printers, in other words, some new information each year.

During her years of producing newsletters—for her own business as well as other companies—Floyd understandably has a lot of advice to give to the aspiring newsletter publisher:

> Your topic has to be narrow enough so that it has PR value and you have some kind of a niche, so pick your subject carefully and make sure you know where to find your prospective buyers, ... Your topic also has to contain a lot of information that is constantly changing and that people have trouble finding on their own. Using my own example, if I were to publish this newsletter as my sole business, it would be tough because it's hard to find newsletter editors.

Since marketing through direct mail is very expensive, Floyd recommends that you pick a subject where the subscribers won't hesitate to spend money to get the kind of information they need. The easiest way is to find a real specialized niche of big business that has money to spend. It makes it easier on you since you don't have to go after as many subscribers. "If I could publish a newsletter that costs $199 a year, I'd need only 200 subscribers and I'd be sitting pretty," she says. "With my newsletter, I'd have to have 2,000 subscribers to pull in the same amount of money. New technologies are a good bet for this, as well as any subject that's really hot and that people are really confused about—like the Internet."

Floyd adds that she thinks people get excited about publishing a newsletter because of the possibility of the get-rich-quick aspect. One newsletter that is regularly held up as an example is *The Tightwad Gazette,* which Floyd says works because it contains a lot of unusual information in each issue. It's wonderfully written, she does a lot of research, and you can tell that she's really worked hard on it. "Plus, she's been a real PR queen," says Floyd. "But still, her success didn't happen overnight. Most people don't realize what it takes, and you have to love your subject enough to do it."

# MARKETING YOUR NEWSLETTER

Marketing is frequently a term that makes a good number of newsletter publishers uncomfortable. Nevertheless, it is one aspect of publishing that they need to know and use intimately in order to survive in the business.

Close your eyes and think: What does marketing mean to you? Most people would think advertising, and not much else. No wonder that it may make you envision images of expensive, glossy ad campaigns on TV and in national magazines, as well as the feeling that there's either something mystical or highly scientific about the ability to draw in customers on the strength of just words and/or pictures.

You don't need a degree in marketing to sell your newsletter effectively. In fact, you're able to sell it better than a professional, mainly because you know your business best. Also, you're not doing what everyone else is doing who's earned an expensive degree in marketing. Sometimes marketing people tend to view marketing with almost a herd mentality: innovative thinking, in terms of coming up with a completely new idea for an ad or publicity campaign, is usually frowned upon simply because it's *too* different. Translated, it means: "How do you know it works?" However, if you're thinking of hiring somebody else to do it just to get the job off your hands, forget about it. Just as no one else will handle your newsletter like you will, so too you're the best person to promote your newsletter. After all the time and money you'll spend on publishing your newsletter, you probably regard it as your baby. So who else is better acquainted with it and therefore better able to convey the attachment and love you have for it to others?

Marketing can actually be fun—you just have to think of it as one of your most creative tasks. In fact, the more creative you are, the more business you'll be able to pull in.

## The Purpose of Marketing

You have a great product: your newsletter. But unless you let people know that you exist, you won't be able to get even one subscriber. Last I heard, ESP is not generally recognized as an effective marketing technique.

"Oh, they'll find out about me somehow," you'll reply. But *how* are they going to hear about your newsletter in the first place? More importantly, how are you going to convince them to sign up for a subscription once they *do* find out about you? With *marketing*.

And how are you going to locate the kinds of people who will be most interested in you newsletter? Through *marketing*.

"My brochure knocks 'em dead." But how are you going to get it in the hands of potential subscribers in the first place? It's great if your brochure and other promotional materials really convey what readers can expect if they sign up for a one-year subscription to your newsletter. However, you must first let them know that you exist before they can send you a check.

The purpose of marketing is to develop and execute a number of different strategies that result in first having prospective subscribers learn about your newsletter, and then convincing them to give you a try.

Always keep in mind that marketing in whatever form will help you to attract new subscribers, and also will help to keep them renewing their subscriptions year after year. As you already know, renewals are the lifeblood of any newsletter, and the best thing about loyal subscribers is the fact that getting them back incurs no additional marketing costs. They're already convinced about the merits of your newsletter, and you don't have to spend time or money trying to sell them on it.

## Defining Your Subscribers

The subject you choose for your newsletter will influence the types of subscribers you're most likely to attract, and also help you to determine the methods you'll use to reach them. For instance, if you want to publish a newsletter about great travel spots in New England, your primary circle of subscribers will come from outside of New England first, a major metropolitan area like New York, and then individuals throughout the rest of the country.

On the other hand, if you publish a newsletter that will provide news and information for people who work in a particular industry, then you already have a good idea of the specific types of subscribers. To reach them, you'll rely on association and other publications that already target this group, but that offer a broader focus than your publication will.

Admittedly, Americans are largely overwhelmed by media messages today, and some research has shown that most people don't pay attention to the majority of the ads they see, anyway. But the messages they *do* notice are the ads that reach out to a specific interest of theirs. If an organization they belong to recommends a certain product—like your newsletter—you can bet they're going to listen and respond.

You should know that you won't be able to reach everybody who would benefit from your newsletter, and even if you could, your message is only one of thousands they see and hear every day. The first step to reaching your customers is to target your ideal subscriber. Even though you should work on attracting subscribers from this initial group simply due to the increase of loyalty they have, your target audience may include potential subscribers in a larger market than you may have imagined. Keeping individual records about your subscribers from the beginning can help you to define your customer even more precisely once you've been running your business for awhile.

Defining who your subscribers are means that you can then narrow down your choice of the avenues you have available to reach them, as well as the methods you use.

---

To help define your subscribers, ask yourself the following questions:

- Who is the most likely type of person to subscribe to your newsletter? Now, describe two other groups of people who would also benefit from your newsletter.

- What other publications do they read? What TV shows and radio programs do they prefer, if any?

- Which organizations do you think they belong to?

- Does their physical location play a role in whether they'd be more likely to subscribe to your newsletter? For example, do they live in a city, the suburbs, or a rural area?

- What is their income range?

- Why will they decide to subscribe to your newsletter?

- What do you think would make them decide *not* to subscribe?

- What do you think their goals are for 5, 10 and 20 years down the road? Will your newsletter help them to reach their goals?

## Finding Prospects

You probably have a good idea of the type of person who is likely to subscribe to your newsletter. Now, how do you go about finding them?

There are numerous ways. You should know, however, that prospects are not the same thing as subscribers. What I'm about to say may take the longest to sink in of anything else I'll say in this book: Even though your newsletter is your baby and everyone around you tells you that it's great and they'd subscribe in a minute, the fact is that only a small percentage of people who write or call for information about your newsletter will actually subscribe—and it might take awhile for them to decide to do so. You must view all prospects as potential customers, and treat them with the same respect as if they were one of your paid subscribers, but you shouldn't be disappointed or surprised when they don't subscribe. Again, think of how many offers you're exposed to each day, or about the sheer number of products that you walk by every time you go to the supermarket. Each and every time, you'll only end up buying and trying a fraction of what's out there, and unfortunately, most of your prospects will regard your newsletter as just another product. That is why it's vital that you spell out exactly how they'll benefit and get much more than their money's worth if they subscribe to your newsletter. We have become a society of fishermen: because there is so much out there to choose from, we must know all there is about everything there is before we make a decision. And even then, there's a little voice in the back of our heads that says, "There's always something better."

Perhaps that is true. But you can help find and convert prospects into paying customers by concentrating on those avenues that your group of defined customers travel on.

Marketing is not always advertising, as many people wrongly assume. In fact, advertising is one of the least effective and most expensive ways to find your prospects.

Think about your defined customers and then consider the places you can find them; use some of the above suggestions for a jumping-off point. You'll undoubtedly be able to think of many more.

## Cloning and Keeping Good Customers

Once you get good customers, hold onto them. Tightly. The good news is, like that shampoo commercial where one person tells two friends and so on down the line, your own good customer knows other people who could also turn out to be good customers for you. After all, word of mouth is probably the most effective kind of marketing there is.

There are a variety of ways you can clone good customers. One way is to ask your current subscribers if they know of other people who would like to receive information about your newsletter. You can include a separate form in your mailings where you ask each subscriber or potential subscriber for names, including space where the subscriber can fill in the names and addresses of friends. Then you can keep track of any subscriptions you receive through this referral system. That way if a friend becomes a subscriber, you can offer the first subscriber a discount off his or her subscription renewal, a technique that will also boost your renewal rate.

I know of one newsletter publisher who sends a discount coupon for 10 percent off a workshop sponsored by the newsletter to current subscribers and encloses an identical coupon for the subscriber to give to a friend.

Treating your repeat customers well each time they stay with you is in essence, a kind of cloning, since they are likely to come back again and again.

The best way to keep your subscribers coming back by renewing and buying your other products is to a) continue to market to your targeted group of customers, and b) be consistent in maintaining the quality of your newsletter and your personal service. After all, one of the reasons why subscribers renew their subscriptions is because they know what to expect. In other words, there will be no surprises.

## Finding the Time

Finding the time to market your newsletter is one of the biggest problems that you'll have when it comes to marketing. I spend 90 percent of my time on marketing and only ten percent on writing. Even when I'm under deadline, I still try to do some marketing work every day. You should, too. The next time you say you don't have time to market your newsletter, consider these tips:

- Because you need to figure out which marketing techniques are bringing in the most subscribers to your newsletter, it's important to ask each subscriber or potential subscriber how he or she heard about the newsletter. This information should then be tabulated to determine your rate of return on paid advertising and where you should plan to spend more of your marketing in the future. Seeing the exact number of dollars that you have pulled in from each of the previous year's advertisements, promotions, and direct mailings will make your media-buying decisions much easier. It also becomes much easier to say *no* to pesky ad salesmen whose publications don't work for you.

- A lot of marketing involves grunt work: stuffing envelopes, making lists, shuffling through ad rate cards. Do this during slow times of the day or night; it's easier to justify when ten other things aren't demanding your attention.

- Examine your slow times, whether it's every Monday or the month of March. Set up the following year's strategies by writing your marketing plan (see Appendix B, on page 205), and then perform maintenance tasks on your weekly slow day.

- Here's a sneaky tip: Ask sales reps from different media to design a media plan for you as a way to get your business. Many reps will do this anyway, of course, giving the biggest percentage of the pie to themselves. Whether you follow through is up to you, but you'll get lots of suggestions and ideas for free and no time spent. Always ask about upcoming promotional tie-in events; frequently you'll get a reduced rate and increased exposure at the event as well.

- Hire someone to carry out your plan, if you truly can't find enough time, or give the responsibility to a staff member. One newsletter publisher hired a PR consultant who was just starting out. She paid the consultant a below-market rate, but tied bonuses into any increased business that resulted from the additional publicity. Some newsletter publishers say that novices are better than experts; although they don't have the contacts, they also don't have a lot of preconceived notions about what's right and what's wrong. With marketing, it's innovation that gets attention.

## Advertising on a Budget

Advertising is a type of marketing where you pay for a certain amount of space or time so you can tell your message to a particular kind of audience. Since you're paying to send the message, you can say anything you want—time or space and money are the only factors that limit you.

Considering these limitations, advertising doesn't really give you much leeway. In fact, because you bought the space, you're obviously selling something, and most people turn right off when someone's trying to sell them something.

Take a look at the ads in your local newspaper or area magazine. What do they look like? How do they make you feel? Is there one in the entire publication that makes you want to drop what you're doing, pick up the phone and call? Probably not. Do the same thing the next time you're watching TV or listening to the radio. Pay close attention to the locally produced ads. Again, do they make you feel excited about whatever it is the advertiser is trying to sell?

I probably can predict what your answer will be. The vast majority of advertising in all media is placed to gain consumer awareness, to let people know that a business exists. And this type of advertising can build business for a newsletter—but very slowly. By the time you're able to measure the results from your advertising program, you may have to go out of business. It's also difficult to measure. How often do you go into a store and say that you heard their radio commercial? Unless the owner is a friend of yours, probably not.

Because advertising is so expensive, you can't waste money to use it just to let people know you're there. Publicity and other more focused marketing tools exist for this reason, and they're also cheap.

No, the only reason you should spend money to advertise is to back up a special promotion or discount that's available for a limited time, or to offer customers a chance to respond to your ad and receive something for their efforts. A toll-free number, a discount coupon, or a special incentive will help you to measure how many people responded, and then who subscribed to your newsletter as the result of your ad. Then you can see if the ad paid for itself, and whether you should try another ad in a later issue of the magazine.

Some newsletter publishers report that they sometimes feel pressure from a newspaper or magazine editor to advertise in exchange for a promise to cover their business in an editorial section of the publication. Though most editors will deny this ever happens, I can tell you that it does exist. However, this form of coercion is most likely to occur at smaller publications, where most or all of their revenue comes from advertising. When the publisher also serves as the editor, you can be sure that any conflict of interest between advertising and editorial departments will frequently be ignored.

If you do decide to advertise, don't settle for the quoted rate. Always ask, "Is that the best you can do?" Especially if the publication is nearing its closing date and there's still ad space left to fill, the sales rep or ad director might let it go at a significant discount. In addition, radio and TV stations and publications frequently offer a special rate to first-time advertisers in the hopes that they'll become regular advertisers. At other times, they'll offer a discount if you advertise in a special section or sponsor a certain program. Again, you should always ask.

Radio and TV advertising don't usually work for newsletter publishers since your primary audience is far too specific for this broad form of marketing to be effective. It's best to focus on print ads in other newsletters, and magazines and newspapers that your target audience reaches. For instance, some of the publications where I advertise *Sticks* include single-state lifestyle magazines where the majority of readers want to live there, but don't. And so *Vermont Magazine, Vermont Life, Montana Magazine*, and a small newsletter called *Vermont Property Owners Report* have brought good results for me.

If you're interested in advertising in a particular publication, call the advertising department and ask for a media kit. You'll probably receive a fat folder with a copy of the magazine, a rate card, and lots of material that shows the demographics of the magazine's readers, comparing the numbers to other similar magazines. Sift through them and take out an ad on a one- or three-time basis in the beginning. Contrary to popular belief and to what ad sales reps say, if an ad doesn't pull for you after a couple of times, your response rate sure isn't going to improve after the seventh insertion. So give it a shot if you think it might work and pull it before you start to lose a significant amount of money.

## Publicity

In the opinion of many newsletter publishers—myself included—publicity is the best kind of marketing you can buy. That's because aside from the initial costs of preparing a press release and contacting the media about your newsletter, publicity is free. And because when a writer writes about your newsletter in a magazine or newspaper, or a reporter spotlights your newsletter on radio or TV, it is considered to be an endorsement of your business by that particular medium. You didn't pay someone to be mentioned as you do whenever you take out an ad, and so the audience will naturally respond more favorably to an unsolicited endorsement than to a paid ad.

An insider aside: editors, writers, and reporters at media large and small will rarely review a newsletter that they don't care for. First off, they don't have the space, and they don't want to waste their own or their audience's time. So, in most cases, if you see a newsletter reviewed in a major magazine, it's likely that the editor and/or author has weeded out less useful newsletters in order to give more space to the one that he or she has chosen.

As with defining your customer, you must also narrow down the media you wish to reach. Many times, your defined customer will select your media for you. For instance, if your defined customers are interested in the subject you cover in your newsletter, they will probably be reading other publications where they can get information on that topic. So what you need to do is contact those same media in the hopes that an editor or writer will see that their readers will benefit from finding out about you. However, if your topic is *too* close, the publication may consider you to be a competitor and permanently freeze you out. This doesn't happen often, however, due to the extremely specialized nature of most newsletters.

First check the name of the editor on the masthead who usually covers the topic that you cover in your newsletter or the writer whose byline regularly appears on stories about your topic. Never contact the editor-in-chief of a large and/or frequent publication, since that person will be far too busy to respond to you. The managing editor or an associate editor is a far better choice.

For instance, going back to the idea of the menu and recipe newsletter for working mothers, if you're looking for subscribers, you can send a press kit to all of the women's and parenting magazines as well as to the food magazines and newspaper editors who handle these subjects. You can also rent mailing lists for this group and then send a direct mail piece their way. Or maybe you'll want to go to a busy supermarket, stand at the exit and hand out a sample issue of your newsletter to exhausted-looking women with children in tow. Better yet, if you're good at making a presentation and at public speaking, maybe you can work out a deal with the supermarket to hold an in-store demonstration using foods the manager wants to push and those that fit in with your menus and recipes. Then the store can include a blurb about your appearance in its weekly advertisements and you can do your own promotion the week before by appearing on local TV and radio talk shows. You can also arrange to be interviewed by your local daily and weekly newspapers. You'll want to arrange to have a reporter cover your demonstration so the next time you schedule an event, people will know to come.

There are literally thousands of ways to promote your newsletter, but I think you get the idea. But before you do any promotion, you'll need a press kit.

## Anatomy of a Press Kit

There are many aspects to marketing a newsletter that scare people off—for some it may be the queasiness of selling yourself, for others, the perceived expense. Perhaps one of the most intimidating is the notion of putting together a press kit. Common reactions range from "I don't have thousands of dollars to invest in some fancy press kit" to "What goes in it?" Another reaction—"Who do I send it to?"—will be the subject of a future column; in fact, it alone could fill a book. In short, this is what goes into a press kit:

- Cover letter
- Press release—usually one, but could be more
- Copy of your newsletter and other promotional material that you hand out to subscribers
- Bio sheet—in other words, some information about *you*
- Press clips
- Glossy black-and-white photo
- A folder to put them in

Why should you have a press kit? To make it easier for a writer or producer to do a story—or even help them make the decision to do a story about your newsletter in the first place. Writers and radio and TV show producers often need more information than can be found in a brochure. For print stories, they'll need a photo that's easily reproduced, which isn't usually possible by reprinting a picture from your brochure.

More importantly, however, a press kit provides this information in a language that media people understand. Even though you may find the format and tone of the material in a press kit to be overly commercial and self-congratulatory, it throws the emphasis on you and your newsletter and presents the facts—the cake, so to speak—so a writer can concentrate on getting the personal details—the frosting—when the time comes to see you in person, or interview you over the phone. Here's a brief rundown of the contents of your press kit:

***Cover Letter.*** This should be brief, usually no more than a page. The first paragraph should consist of one sentence, and that line should be enticing and draw the reader in. I frequently like to word it in the form of a question. In the next paragraph, answer the question and then tell how your newsletter will help the editor's readers improve their lives in some way, whether it's to save time or help them to relax. Then tell why you're writing to the editor at this particular time, whether it is to alert the media to a special event or to provide them with an introduction and background material on your newsletter.

Then provide a few story suggestions that fall into that particular media's genre and that don't wholly focus on you.

***Press Release.*** This should cover the four Ws of news writing— who, where, when and why—and, of course, how, again with an enticing lead followed by brief paragraphs that are to the point and provide the media with background information. Mention should also be made of the timeliness of your topic.

***Sample Issue of Your Newsletter.*** This will let the writer see your newsletter through a subscriber's eyes.

***Bio Sheet.*** This essentially is your résumé in prose format. Sometimes an editor or producer will decide to do a story on your newsletter based on your own personal history, so it helps if you play up something about your life that is unusual or follows current trends in your story. In fact, start right off the bat by making it your headline. For instance, if you've always dreamed of publishing your own newsletter and either struggled through a high-paying prestigious job for a number of years in order to save up the money, say so, and say it early on.

***Past Press Clips.*** Frequently, journalists are like cattle: They won't cover a story unless somebody else has done it first. Contrary to popular belief, it's not difficult to get press—in many cases, all you have to do is ask for it. If you're new in town or if you've done something different for your newsletter, that's news and you should contact a reporter about it even if you haven't been written up in the past. Try it; you'll see how easy it is. Try the business editor at your local daily or the features editor at your local community weekly paper for a start.

***Glossy Black-and-White Photo.*** Though a newspaper will frequently send a photographer to take a picture to accompany a story about you and your newsletter, some of the smaller papers don't have the budget or the time, and they'll usually publish whatever you send them. A 5 × 7 or 8 × 10 glossy black-and-white photograph—usually a picture of the front of you sitting at your computer taken at a slight angle—will do. Don't send color prints or slides unless they're specifically requested. You may want to enclose another shot of you—perhaps a full front shot showing you holding a copy of your newsletter—but it's not necessary.

***A Folder to Put Them In.*** Nothing fancy here, just a plain folder with pockets you can stash all of the above in neatly. Some newsletters put a label on the front that lists the name of their newsletter along with the name of their publishing company, their town, state, and phone number but it's not necessary.

On occasion, a reporter or producer will ask for individual pieces from your press kit. This is typical, so don't be offended that they won't want to see your entire masterpiece.

And that's what a press kit should be: a capsule of your business, designed to make members of the media think enough of you and your business to want to tell their readers or listeners about you. And this, of course, is the best kind of advertising you could get.

## Pricing Your Newsletter

This is always a sticky situation. There are some people who will always find it extremely difficult to ask other people for money, and as a result, either undercharge or overcharge. Both scenarios will keep subscribers away.

The price you set for a subscription will have a lot to do with your specific audience and whether you are publishing your newsletter for a consumer or business market.

You've undoubtedly heard of the newsletters that charge hundreds, even thousands of dollars for a year's subscription, and that people eagerly subscribe to the publication for the information they can receive from it. These newsletters usually cover very specialized fields and appeal to people high up the rung in a company, or in a field of only several thousand people in the entire country. One example of this type of newsletter would be a weekly two-page publication for petroleum engineers at oil companies. The newsletter is faxed at 8:00 A.M. sharp every Monday morning. Another example is aimed toward production executives at high-volume snack food companies. This type of newsletter is usually published by a former specialist in the field or a consultant who knows that particular business inside out, and whose name and reputation is respected by the small audience in the industry. For such specialized information, the newsletter publisher can easily charge $1,000 a year for a subscription. Even if there are only a 100 loyal subscribers, they are still pulling in a good income after expenses.

I'll venture a guess that most of you reading this book won't be dealing in subscription prices at these levels. Consumer newsletters rarely go above $50 a year, and that's for a monthly. Many consumers are reluctant to pay even that amount for a newsletter basically because they are unfamiliar with the concept. They compare the sheer content of a newsletter ("only 8 pages every other month?") with a monthly magazine with 200 glossy four-color pages that costs only $14.97 for a year's subscription, and they immediately turn up their noses at the idea of a newsletter. I've had people abruptly cancel their subscriptions upon receiving their first issue of my newsletter simply because they thought they were getting a magazine, even though I am always clear in my advertising and other promotional material that these are *newsletters* and not magazines. Be prepared for this, because it will happen.

Because of this, you may find that you need to do a little bit of education from time to time. Stressing that your news-letter is "packed with information designed to save you $800 a year/lose weight/lower your blood pressure/get you a better job" and the fact that this information is not available any-where else in such detail in one publication will help convert some skeptics. For the others, I strongly suggest that you offer a full money-back guarantee to your publication.

You heard me right. A full money-back guarantee—or at least granting money back on undelivered issues—will serve to remove some of the worry from a prospective subscriber. It also means that you are standing behind your newsletter and the value of the information you put in it. The secret is that if you have a good product and deliver what you promise in advertising and your other promotional literature, it's a sure thing that only a tiny fraction of your readers will take you up on it. By the time their first-year subscription is up, it's likely that they won't remember your guarantee. If they are dissatis-fied with your newsletter for some reason, you'll see it in your renewal rates, and not in the number of people who write in for a full refund.

This is a good time to discuss the types of subscriptions you should offer. Some newsletters offer two types of subscrip-tions in their solicitations: six months, and a full year. This, in my opinion, is a big mistake. Even if the price per issue is cheaper with the one-year subscription, more people will choose the six-month option as a way to test you out. This is to your disadvantage, since you will spend the same amount of time and money processing each subscription, but in a longer subscription, since you're dealing in volume, you'll come out of it with more profit. For instance, charging $36 for a year's subscription to a bimonthly newsletter with your cost per newsletter for postage, editing, writing and printing at approximately 50 cents, offering a half-year subscription at $20 allows you to clear $18.50 from that subscription before subtracting your considerable promotional costs as well as your overhead. On a one-year subscription, your costs will be $3, leaving you with $33 from each subscription, earning you $15 more from each subscription with a minuscule amount of extra work, i.e. mailing out additional issues each time you mail out one.

One area that I've dealt with many times and have finally come up with a definitive policy for is the subject of sample issues. Should you send them out free, or should you charge for them? Some newsletter publishers swear by the value of sending out free sample copies to those who ask for them, or who respond to an ad where free sample issues are mentioned. I disagree, at least with consumer newsletters where the subscriber has to come up with a subscription fee that may seem inordinately high, again, as compared to fat cheaper publications like magazines and newspapers. When I've sent out free sample copies to people who want to have a look before they subscribe, I've always lost money on the deal. First of all, one issue is not enough for most people to judge whether or not a year's subscription would be valuable to a reader. After all, I'd be hard-pressed to find a subscriber to any of my newsletters who will find everything in one issue of the newsletter to be valuable to them. This is only possible to judge after a full year. This, of course, will then be reflected in your renewal rate. Also, after receiving the sample issue, people will frequently ask themselves if they think it's worth $6, or whatever fraction of the subscription price it amounts to. Most people, unfortunately, will say no. I've also had one particularly cantankerous local newspaper reporter graph it out like that in print: "Folks, I don't believe that this information is worth six bucks an issue." Of course, I later bumped into him and informed him that the particular newsletter for which he had predicted a quick demise had more than 1,000 satisfied subscribers who were quite happy to pay six bucks an issue. This is not an isolated instance, as jealousy from the media will sometimes rear its quite unattractive head.

Finally, in terms of setting the price of your newsletter itself, it is possible to experiment through direct mail by sending out a direct mail piece that is identical except for the price. You can also test the price on a per-issue basis. Magazines regularly offer this rate via subscription and can attract subscribers by offering an issue for less than a dollar. Your subscription offer may pale by comparison, since you may be charging six dollars or more per issue. One way to capitalize on this is to guarantee to offer at least $100 worth of information in each issue—and you'll get this valuable advice for only six dollars a month!

By necessity, consumer newsletters are priced lower than business-oriented newsletters. As I've already mentioned, consumer newsletters tend to be published less frequently. Because of the great resistance to paying a lot of money for a skinny eight-page newsletter, you'll have to look toward volume for your profit.

I've seen one-year subscription rates for an eight-page bimonthly newsletter set anywhere from $12 up to $100 and even more. I think the ideal range is anywhere from $24 to just under $50. Business newsletters, on the other hand, can run from $20 for a quarterly all the way up to several thousand dollars for a weekly publication sent via fax. Most business publications, however, range from around $50 up to $200.

Nonround numbers—$98, $113, $165—seem to be popular, though I'm not sure of the reasoning behind them. The average range is from $75 for a monthly to $150 for a two- to four-page weekly.

While the subscription rates you'll pull in should be your bread and butter, ancillary products like Special Reports, seminars, books, and tapes can reap great profits. For one, you produce them once—or buy them at wholesale rates from other publishers—and the more you sell the lower your cost per unit remains. Special Reports of four to ten pages can cost about a dollar a page, audio tapes of special programs can be priced from $10 to $25, and the profit margin if you sell books by other publishers can be as high as 40 percent, as long as you charge extra for shipping and handling.

Though seminars can be a lot of work, you can bring in extra income from current subscribers—and boost their faith in you—and attract potential customers who may buy some of your products and also subscribe to your newsletter. A seminar can be anything from a 90-minute evening program held in a rented room at the local YMCA to a full-fledged week-long convention, complete with a full roster of experts in your field who give workshops, a trade show with hundreds of exhibitors, and other special social programs for attendees.

Some seminar organizers charge an admission fee—customary when the seminar lasts a day or more—while others let people in for free in the hopes that they'll subscribe to their newsletter or sign up for a longer seminar a week or two down the road that *does* charge a fee. The custom is to offer a discount if an attendee signs up well in advance of the workshop, and to charge full price at the door, or up to a week before the seminar begins. In any case, the show producer doesn't expect to make money off the admission fees, but instead hopes to raise enough money to cover the cost of the room rental as well as the money spent to promote the event.

To get a better idea of the range of seminar prices, check what others in your field are doing. As a basic rule, however, for a consumer-oriented show, anything more than $20 at the door will greatly decrease the response. Ten dollars is more like it, with a free bag of products donated by some of the exhibitors and workshop leaders.

For a seminar that is aimed toward the owner of a small business, I've seen the fees range from $45 to $150. Where anything goes is at shows for professionals and owners of larger businesses. The fee per day can range from $150 to $500 a day—but remember, in many of these cases, it is the attendee's employer who will pick up the tab.

Set your price on the products you sell, but be willing to play around with it a little if the results you want don't immediately materialize. Keep in mind that in some cases—particularly newsletters for business people—if the price is too low, potential readers may be turned off because they may perceive it to have no value.

## Fulfilling Subscriptions

It's easy to design a system where you can keep track of subscribers and when their subscriptions are going to expire so you can begin the process of getting them to renew.

I use a regular database program, putting one piece of information into each column like name, address, and expiration date. For the expiration date, I use the number of the last issue of their subscription. For instance, if their subscription will expire with the #14 issue, I insert #14 on the top line. Then I merge my database with the mailing label function to print the labels out on 1 × 2⅝ inch label sheets—30 to a page—which I then peel off and apply to each envelope.

Here's what a typical label looks like:

```
#12
Janet Kaplan
Tweed River Inn
POB 280
Tweed, OH 45222
```

With many computer programs you can also customize each label to send a specific message, say, to every subscriber you have in New York State, or another line that tells them that this is their last issue.

When a new subscription comes in, here's what I do:

1. I enter their name and address into the subscriber database. In an additional column in the database, I list where they learned about my newsletter.

2. If the subscription comes in during the first half of the issue date—for instance, during November for a November/December issue date, I'll send out that issue and address the envelope by hand. If the subscription comes in during the second half of the issue date, I'll usually wait until the next issue to send out the first issue of their subscription.

3. I mark the expiration date on the outside of the subscriber's original envelope and store it and all other written correspondence in a file.

4. I endorse the check and clip it to a deposit slip. If the subscriber pays by credit card, I'll fill out a charge slip with the subscriber's credit card number and phone number and list exactly what was ordered, and set it aside to transmit it to the bank with a batch of other slips at the end of the day.

5. If the subscription is a gift, I'll enclose a card telling the new subscriber who the gift is from, and I'll record the gift giver in another column in the subscriber's entry in the database.

6. Once a week, I copy the entire subscription file to a floppy disk and store it in a fireproof box.

I also usually send new subscribers a handwritten note thanking them for their order. If a question was asked that I can answer briefly, then I'll include a short note about the query as well. Most people are surprised to receive a personal response when they never expected one, and I've found that this small gesture goes a long way toward building a roster of loyal customers. In fact, I've even had some subscribers who have written me back to thank me for my personal reply.

Many times, a new subscriber will ask me if I have ever written an article on a specific subject or if I sell a Special Report on another topic. Some newsletter publishers have a pre-printed sheet they can send to the subscriber as a response, but since they are already subscribers, I refer them to that section of my newsletter where I list all of the ancillary products that are offered for sale.

I follow a similar process whenever I receive an order for books or Special Reports. I *always* hold onto the initial correspondence in case a problem arises later.

After you've been publishing your newsletter for about a year, you'll have to delete some of your subscribers while making changes to those that remain as your subscribers begin to renew their subscriptions and others allow them to lapse.

When you receive a renewal order from a subscriber, all you have to do is change the expiration date in that subscription's record to the new last issue. However, when subscribers decide not to renew their subscription, you'll need to remove their names from your subscription list. You shouldn't delete them, however; instead, create a new file of subscribers who have failed to renew. You'll learn how to win back a good percentage of your former subscribers with persistence and patience. See the section on Renewals for more information.

## Accepting Phone Orders

Whatever you can do to make it easier for people to subscribe to your newsletter, you should do it. One way is to set up a toll-free number that people can call directly and subscribe. A toll-free number is very affordable these days; usually your local phone company or long-distance phone service can set you up for a basic monthly rate of $10-15. You pay for each call that comes in, which I've seen range from 18 to 30 cents a minute, depending upon the time of day as well as the region of the country that your caller is phoning from.

However, I must caution you that a toll-free number is pretty much useless if you do not also accept credit cards like MasterCard and Visa. Many times, especially for a consumer-oriented newsletter, a subscription to your newsletter will be considered to be an impulse buy. In most cases, that involves whipping out a piece of plastic to pay for it. If people call your toll-free line expecting to place an order, only to be told that they'll have to write out a check, address an envelope, put a stamp on it, and put it in a mailbox—which also increases the length of time before they'll receive their first issue—most people won't even bother, thinking that it's too much work. Of course, it isn't, not from your viewpoint, anyway, but I can guarantee that you'll lose a significant amount of revenue if you: a) don't have an 800 number, and b) don't accept credit cards. With L.L. Bean offering 24-hour operators and shipping your order out the next day via Federal Express, the expectations of shoppers everywhere have been raised. This will be to your disadvantage if you don't accept credit cards on a toll-free number. Of course, it may not drive you out of business, but I've published newsletters with and without credit cards, and my revenues with credit cards are twice that without.

For more information on how you can receive credit card merchant status in order to accept credit card orders, see Chapter 8.

## Should You Accept Advertising?

This is one of the stickiest subjects among newsletter publishers everywhere. Purists who are against advertising state that a newsletter's sole function is to provide *news* and not serve as a promotional vehicle for other companies. And then I've seen newsletters that are more than 50 percent ads.

I'd say that at least 50 percent of newsletters today accept some form of advertising, whether it's a small classified or display ad, or an information sheet that another company pays you to insert into a copy of your newsletter. Some spread the advertising throughout the publication while others restrict it to a couple of pages in the back, a mixture of display and classified.

I accept ads in my own newsletters—I think that it adds a touch of professionalism to the advertisers in the eyes of my readers. Since a company is advertising in my newsletter, it adds some credibility. My advertisers have also told me that the response rate on a per-subscriber basis is much higher than they could get in any other kind of media. Again, since a newsletter is so specialized, this makes sense.

At this time, I don't actively solicit advertisers; they come to me after reading about my newsletter or hearing about it from a subscriber. I have actively solicited advertising in the past with a cover letter, an ad rate sheet, and a sample of the newsletter, all of which is necessary if you want to pursue advertising. Renting lists of businesses that may appeal to your readers is one way to go about it.

Most business-oriented newsletters with a circulation of 5,000 or less charge a pittance for advertising. This is another reason why I think accepting advertising increases the reputation of a publication, since it's probably viewed as a service to readers and not as a great money-maker. I charge 50 cents a word with a 20-word minimum, or $15 per column inch for a display ad. My advertisers tell me that I'm too cheap, given the response that they get, but it's not something I have the desire to go after. If it were, I'd probably be publishing a magazine, and not a newsletter.

## Selecting the Frequency of Your Newsletter

This is a tough one. You may want to publish a monthly newsletter, but may envision that to publish monthly and still keep your subscription rate at a reasonable level is difficult. In addition, since most newsletter publishers start out by doing most if not all of the writing themselves in the beginning, monthly publication can be a quick ticket to burnout before the first year is up.

Yet most subscribers feel that bimonthly—and especially quarterly—isn't often enough for them. Then you hear about the weekly newsletters and wonder how they do it; and understand perfectly that they're earning every penny of their several-hundred dollar subscription fee.

I've always published bimonthly consumer newsletters because I felt if I was producing twice as much material I wouldn't have the time to market the newsletter, and then where would I get my subscribers from? If the subscribers have to wait a little longer between issues, I figure it makes them that much more eager for your publication when it does arrive. It also makes me much more aware that I have to produce a high-quality publication each time out, instead of writing off an issue here and there because I was too burned out to put enough time into it.

Some publishers handle this dilemma by publishing half the normal newsletter twice as often. For instance, if they were—or planned to—publish an eight-page bimonthly newsletter, instead they publish a four-page newsletter once a month. The problem with this arrangement is that your postage costs double since you're mailing out a newsletter twice as often. Also, since an eight-page newsletter is just under an ounce, it costs the same amount to send a smaller publication. Since you still must basically start from scratch with each newsletter, even though you have fewer pages to fill, I think you'd reach the burnout point quicker still than a publisher who keeps to a bimonthly schedule. Of course, if you can hire a full- or part-time employee from the beginning, this is less of a concern to you, but it is still an important consideration, since you are managing the production of a monthly publication. The call is yours.

For professional newsletters, however, bimonthly is too long of a lag for people who need new information to help them run their businesses. For my newsletter, *Travel Marketing Bulletin*, which goes to owners of small travel businesses, I didn't want to publish monthly, but bimonthly was out of the question. So I devised a nine-times-a-year publishing schedule that goes like this: January, February, March, May, June, July, September, October, and November, shipping three months, two of which—August and December—tend to be busy in this industry—while the other month—April, tends to be slow. Another time, I designed an eight-times a year newsletter publishing schedule as January, February, March/April, May, June/July, August, September/October, and November/December.

When setting the frequency of your newsletter, be truthful about what you can handle with the resources you have at hand as well as what your readers would prefer. Frequently, as newsletters become more popular both among publishers and readers, a publisher can afford to hire help and therefore increase the frequency.

## Finding Writers for Your Newsletter

Sooner or later, many newsletter publishers discover that they would prefer not to do all of the writing for the newsletter themselves. Indeed, some know this at the very beginning and begin to arrange to have some or all of the articles written by outside contributors, or an editor who works for you on either an in-house or freelance basis. How do you go about finding writers in the first place?

Look for experts in your field who would view a byline in your newsletter as a credit to their reputation and expertise. For instance, with the nutrition newsletter, you could ask around your area for the names of nutritionists and dietitians who work with busy working mothers—but it doesn't even need to get that specific. Any nutritionist with a decent background and a desire to provide specific information within the forum of your newsletter would be a good bet. Call local, state, and national professional organizations for some referrals.

Another good place to start is at your bookstore for the names of authors who have written books on your subject, and who may want to sell more and expand their reputation. The advantage of this is that they already have written materials that can be easily edited and adapted to the format of your newsletter. It's possible that in lieu of payment, you could offer to include ordering information for their book or consultation services at the end of each article they write, and so increase their revenue and build up their mailing lists for their own pursuits.

When you contact the various professional organizations, you can also ask if you can place a notice in their association newsletter that you're looking for writers, but the result may be that you're flooded with inquiries. I'd also caution you against contacting writer's organizations and magazines. It's been my experience that you'll receive many submissions that are totally inappropriate for your publication. Many that I receive, even though I do no formal solicitations for writers, is what many editors in my position call "Me 'n Joe" stories. Poorly written with no imagination, they tend to be boring monologues that describe in excruciating detail what the correspondent did and felt along the way of some particular experience—with absolutely nothing left out. I sometimes reply with a terse note penciled on the sender's letter—"Not what we're looking for." I also inform the writer that sample copies are $6, should he or she wish to get an idea of the market he or she is writing for. Needless to say, if the writer does not enclose a self-addressed stamped envelope, the letter and manuscript are headed right for the circular file.

You'll also receive letters from prospective writers to request writer's guidelines. Basically, this typically one-page sheet tends to spell out who your readers are, some of the articles and columns you like to feature in the newsletter, average word length of each article, and the amount of money you will pay. Some newsletter publishers also like to make clear what they're not looking for, á la "Me 'n Joe" stories or other topics that many would-be writers for your newsletter may tend to come up with first—in other words, those that are too obvious. Sometimes, but not always, seeing one sample issue is enough to greatly reduce the number of highly inappropriate queries.

Next, the problem of what to pay for articles. Some newsletters pay nothing and figure the prestige of writing for them is enough. At the other extreme are newsletter publishers who overpay—albeit very few—either because they can afford to, or because they want someone else to write the articles.

The happy medium, of course, is somewhere in the middle. Although you probably can't pay much in the beginning, I think you should try to pay something—at least a token $25—to show you value the writers as vital contributors to your publication. You can either pay them when you accept the article or upon publication—when the issue of your newsletter with their story in it comes out. For my newsletter, I pay on publication just to keep my business more organized. For one, the lead time between when the article has to be written and when the issue comes out can be the day before the issue goes to the printer, so upon acceptance actually turns out to be upon publication. Because I send all the issues out at once—to subscribers, advertisers, review copies to the press, and to my writers—it helps me to remember to send the writer a copy. Otherwise, with the chaos that's endemic to any newsletter publishing operation, as you'll undoubtedly discover, sometimes the little things fall by the wayside if you don't have them firmly integrated into some kind of system.

Another method of finding writers is through the professional writers' organizations, like the National Writers Union and the American Society of Journalists and Authors, both based in New York City. However, it is almost inevitable that you can't afford to have them write for your newsletter, especially when you're first starting out, since the majority of the ASJA's members make their living full-time from freelance writing for magazines and books. It would take a lot of $25 articles before they'd be able to live comfortably.

Another problem with writers, no matter where you find them, is the fact that many have no idea what it's like to write in the tight, newsy style that most newsletters require due to space constraints. So even if you've convinced the most prominent authority in your field to write for your newsletter, be prepared to edit with a heavy hand.

## Renewals

Whenever two or more newsletter publishers get together, guess what question they ask each other most frequently?

"What's your renewal rate?"

Convincing people that they should subscribe to your newsletter for the first time actually isn't that difficult. It's a good bet that they're excited about receiving their first issue. And like any new thing, the anticipation of receiving a new product by mail that covers a topic they're intensely interested in, is part of the reason why they'll order a year's worth of your newsletter in the first place. Getting those same people to continue to renew their subscription year after year is the tough part.

The reason why a high renewal rate is so sought after by newsletter publishers is that most publishers spend a lot of money promoting and marketing, so the rate you end up paying to convince each subscriber to give you a try is high. For instance, say you buy an ad in a magazine for $300, a low rate by most standards. If you get 20 responses to your $30-a-year newsletter, you'll make $300, after subtracting the cost of the ad. This isn't particularly bad since there are many ads out there that don't make back the cost of featuring them.

Look at how much money you had to spend to get each subscriber: $300 divided by 20 is $15. That means you've spent $15 for each subscriber. Then subtract your printing and postage costs to send each issue, and while you're still making money, your profits go down.

On the other hand, look at the money you'll earn from a renewing subscriber. You may spend the price of a stamp on a renewal letter. A few dimes or less—depending if you send it first class or bulk rate—is a lot better than spending $15 to get each subscriber. The best part is you didn't need to convince them of the value they'd get from your newsletter, since they already know.

Deep-pocketed magazine publishers have made it difficult for newsletter publishers to get renewals without sinking a lot of money into printing and postage. Fat, glossy, niche magazines rely on each subscriber so they can tout their circulation figures to advertisers. The advertisers will spend more money on an ad because the rates are set according to the number of subscribers who have paid to receive that magazine, in addition to people who buy it off the newsstand. They have a vested interest in boosting their numbers, especially since most magazines customarily claim three to four times the number of actual readers—both newsstand and paid subscribers—because the publisher typically assumes a pass-along rate of three or four readers. This is usually an exaggerated figure.

Because they have so much riding on renewals, their annual subscription rates are cheaper. Since their budgets are larger, they can afford to bombard their readers with up to ten renewal notices, sometimes making progressively better offers as the number of renewal notices increases. Sometimes persistence will wear down even disgruntled former readers, but you don't have that luxury.

What works for me in getting renewals is the following:

1. With the subscriber's next-to-last issue, I'll enclose a pre-printed note informing them that their subscription will run out with the next issue and they should renew now. If they do chose to renew at this time, I'll reward them with a premium, usually a Special Report or perhaps a book. If they renew for more than one year, they get a better deal since I take $7 off the price of a two-year subscription. Instead of two years at $36 each, I charge $65 for two years.

2. With the last issue, I repeat my offer, and remind them of what they'll be missing if they let their subscription lapse. I also give them a hint of the can't-miss stories that are going to appear in upcoming issues, just to give them another reason to renew.

3. About a month after their subscription has expired and they haven't renewed, I'll send a letter that says, in essence, we miss you. At this point, some newsletter publishers chop a few bucks off the subscription price,

but I caution against it because it can backfire with future renewals. Subscribers will wait to renew if they know they can save money doing it. Besides, shaving a few bucks off the price usually isn't much of an incentive.

Some newsletter publishers will also send a humorous postcard that pokes fun at subscribers' laziness and at the same time, underlines the value of what they've been missing. Sometimes this is enough to bring a subscriber back.

In any case, you should continue to mail *We Want You Back* subscription offers to your expired subscribers as often as you can afford it. Again, several bulk-rate renewal letters are cheaper than spending $15 to get a new subscriber. While you wonder why you regularly get bombarded by countless renewal letters from publishers that you think you have no use for, a poorly kept secret in publication circles is that no matter what you offer, your own list of expired subscribers will always bring better results than a list of similar people who have shown they would be interested in your newsletter, that you rent or assemble on your own. This is because, like I've already said, your former subscribers are already convinced of the merits of your newsletter. All they need is a little nudging or some time to get their credit card under its credit limit.

Another thing you can do is mail an offer of just your ancillary products, offering a 10 percent discount if they order more than just a couple of books or Special Reports. Also include a space on the order form where they can check off to renew their subscriptions. You may be surprised at the results, since many will figure as long as they're ordering these products from you, they might as well order another year's subscription as well.

To paraphrase a famous bard: Never underestimate the quirkiness of your readers. Keep on them, and eventually you'll win many of them back.

## Direct Mail

In addition to a brochure, which you'll send out when a potential subscriber calls or writes for information, you'll need to develop a direct mail package if you plan to rent mailing lists and send information that's the equivalent of a cold call. Some newsletter publishers send the direct mail piece to people who call, but I think a brochure will suffice since by making the first move, the potential subscriber doesn't need to be sold on the benefits of subscribing to your newsletter. And it will save you some money, since the printing and postage costs for the typical direct mail package is incredibly expensive.

A direct mail piece needs to be more extensive by its very nature, since most people don't respond to an unsolicited direct mail offer unless the literature answers all of their questions.

There are hundreds of books that will tell you how to write and design an effective direct mail package, but at the very least, here's what you'll need:

- *Letter:* It can range from one to four pages, or even more. Experts say the longer the letter, the higher your response will be. Remember that your readers must feel comfortable sending money or a credit card number to a company they've never dealt with before.

- *Order form:* Make it easy for people to respond. Look at other order forms or the subscription cards you find in many magazines. Then make sure that it fits in a . . .

- *Reply envelope:* I usually use a #9 envelope with my return address printed on it so that subscribers can easily slip the card into it. Some publishers arrange to pay for the postage, but this can become expensive. I've found that people don't object to using their own stamp, but some mail order experts assert that it cuts down on the response.

- *An envelope to put it all in:* I put my return address in the upper left-hand corner with a teaser of some kind in the lower left. This brief phrase should entice the recipient to open it up, which is sometimes a great challenge, especially if you send your package bulk rate.

With these four pieces, you'll have a bare-bones direct mail package. If you can add a sheet that provides even more information about your newsletter—perhaps on colored paper—again, your response rate should increase.

## Promotional Materials for Your Newsletter

Your brochure is the most important part of your marketing arsenal. Many times, it will be the first impression that a potential subscriber will see of your newsletter. As such, it has the ability to make or break your business. Once you're set on the design for your brochure, all of your other promotional materials—stationery, business cards, and advertisements—should follow the same theme and look.

Your brochure can be fancy or simple. I like three-panel brochures with a question on the front panel and lots of information on the inner panels that will show the recipient how your newsletter can help them to solve some of their problems.

Since most newsletters are simple in design—as compared to magazines—their brochures tend to be simpler, with one color of ink on textured ivory or cream-colored paper, and not glossy brochures with a number of four-color photos.

As for print advertising—I don't know of any case in which radio or TV advertising would work for a newsletter—tailor your ad to the publication, but make it just a bit different so that it stands out. And since you're limited to a small space anyway, ads always work best if you can spur the reader onto taking action *now,* preferably with a phone call to your 800 number. In the ad copy, don't just tell what you're about, tell potential subscribers how subscribing to your newsletter will improve their life in some way.

## The Seven Most Commonly Asked Questions by New Newsletter Publishers

*1. How do I track which ads pull?*

A: Most businesses ask new prospects where they heard about their company, but frequently people will give the name of a wrong magazine—or one that doesn't even exist. Classify each ad and article with its own department number and track your responses. Then gear your future advertising and publicity plans toward those markets that pull best.

*2. Marketing is my Achilles' heel. I know I should do it, but I'm not sure how to go about it. What can I do?*

A: Marketing is a scary thing for many people, but if you spend an uninterrupted period of time each week just on marketing, your business will grow. Either set aside a five-hour period once a week—and hire someone to answer the phone for the afternoon—or set a goal to accomplish one marketing task each day. For instance, send out letters to five people who have just become new subscribers to thank them, or send notes and information to five different editors, writers, or producers.

*3. I think my business appeals mostly to women. How do I target them?*

A: Gear your promotional material toward the market you want to reach. Then market your business with an eye on two audiences: the general and the specific. General marketing will reach members of your desired audience who don't read specialized publications. The specific markets are smaller, but in most cases, they're more responsive to your message. And the fact that you're marketing toward women has a real benefit: One rule in marketing is if you reach the women, the family will follow.

4. *Help! What do I do when the media calls?*

A: Drop everything and smile. Treat them like royalty while you make it appear as though it's business as usual.

5. *How do I set my marketing budget as a percentage of total sales?*

A: Customarily, businesses should set aside anywhere from 5 percent to 25 percent of gross sales to invest in marketing and promotion. For newsletter publishers who are just getting their businesses off the ground, however, even 5 percent can be too much. Instead, you should put the bulk of your limited energies and dollars into creative, inexpensive marketing strategies like publicity.

6. *How come the same newsletters get written up in the big magazines over and over again?*

A: These publishers spend a good deal of time cultivating their media contacts. Even if a reporter just calls for a brochure, the person in charge of marketing adds them to the media list and regularly sends out personalized notes about new features or programs that concern the newsletter.

7. *Can I really negotiate for better ad rates off the rate card?*

A: Yes, especially if the issue closing date is nearing and there's still empty space to fill. Ask the ad director for special rates for new advertisers, frequency discounts, cheaper special sections, and if you can delay your payment until the issue goes to press. It *is* possible to save up to 75 percent on advertising. Most people simply don't ask, and end up paying full price.

**Action Guidelines**

✔ Analyze the types of subscribers you'd like to reach.

✔ Think about the places you're most likely to find them.

✔ Continually market to subscribers who have let their subscriptions lapse.

✔ Don't consider advertising to be your only form of marketing.

## Newsletter Publisher Profile

### Peter Baylies
### *At-Home Dad*

Peter Baylies of Andover, Massachusetts, was a casualty of the downsizing and cutbacks going on everywhere in the computer industry. He was laid off from Digital Equipment, and though he was looking for a job, he resigned himself to staying at home and caring for his nine-month-old son, John.

He did start thinking about starting a home business, however, and heard about the infamous *Tightwad Gazette* newsletter. "I thought about doing another newsletter on the subject, but the publisher had done such a good job and I had also heard about 20 or 30 copycat newsletters, so I ruled that one out," he said. "The next thing I thought of was doing a newsletter about David Letterman. Then I thought I should do something I know a lot about." He glanced over at his son, and the rest is history.

*At-Home Dad* is a newsletter about men who stay home with their children. Though he had worked at a computer company, he needed to familiarize himself with the basics about newsletter publishing. The first issue of *At-Home Dad* was filled mostly with stories about his experiences, but he also went online to look for others on the bulletin boards that were aimed toward parents. Baylies sent e-mail to some of the bulletin boards telling people he was looking for material, and he was able to balance out his first and subsequent issues.

He struck gold with his first issue, sending a sample issue and press kit to editors at 250 newspapers and magazines across the country. Among others, *Woman's Day* responded by writing up a small blurb in the magazine, which resulted in

1,000 responses and 100 subscriptions from readers of the magazine. He also got calls from freelance writers who had seen the blurb and who also wrote stories about the newsletter. He appeared on Marilu Henner's TV show, which added to his subscription base.

*At-Home Dad* is a quarterly newsletter, a decision that Baylies put a lot of thought into. "The reason I made it a quarterly was because I spent most of my time looking after my son," he said. "I knew publishing a monthly newsletter was a lot of work, and frankly, I didn't have the time. I also thought that I'd have less good material if I published the newsletter more often."

Even though Baylies has had great success with media placement, he says that his biggest challenge is finding and getting publicity, from figuring out who to write to to knowing what to say to reporters when they call. "It's almost like going out and getting a job, since I spend a lot of time on my résumé—my press kit—and then I'll get an interview," he said. "And I'm always being interviewed. You should remember that what may start out as a little blurb in the mind of the reporter may actually grow into a feature article as you continue to talk.

"A lot of the reporters I've dealt with are a little bit lazy, since they want the phone numbers of at-home dads to talk to as well as statistics and other information. So whenever I get a call from a reporter, I tell them that I have the names of several dads in their area who they can interview for their story, giving it a bit of local color."

How did he get the names? When the *Woman's Day* story came out, he didn't get a lot of subscribers, but he got a lot of names, which he categorized by state so that whenever a reporter calls, he could supply names. Now, since his subscription list has grown to 450 names, he gives reporters the names of his readers. Since his readers are usually happy to be interviewed by the media, Baylies enjoys an extra bonus of a higher renewal rate.

He also conducted a survey of his subscribers that showed that fathers in general are taking more care of their kids. He took the information and assembled it into a press release, and sent it out to promote the newsletter again. He also plans special Father's Day promotions and says that some women have subscribed to the newsletters for their husbands, hoping they would take the hint and decide to stay at home with the kids. Baylies says that he will capitalize on that niche as well.

He adds that what makes his job particularly difficult is that his audience is hard to find, since there's no mailing list that exists for them, aside from the names he's collected. The advice he has for other newsletter publishers is to be obsessed with their subject. "The people who do well at publishing a newsletter love what they're doing and are already really good at it," he said. "If you just go out looking for a subject it won't work, because you won't be motivated.

"You should know a lot about what you're doing, because your subscribers can tell if you don't know what you're doing," he adds. "There are a lot of newsletters out there that are nothing more than filler and they don't have much to do with what the newsletter is about. You will discover that your readers will know and respond accordingly."

# MANAGING YOUR FINANCES

F inances, ugh. Why can't I just publish my newsletter and be content to know that the financial end will take care of itself?

Because if all you do is deposit checks and credit card orders and write checks to pay your bills, you may never know if you're earning a profit or not. This can lead to your newsletter business first stumbling, and then going down the tubes without you ever knowing the reason why.

It's not too difficult to keep a handle on the various financial aspects of running your newsletter publishing business. As with determining your day-to-day operating procedures, if you take some time with it now, you'll probably end up spending much less time on it down the road.

## Profits and Losses

One important way to gauge how your newsletter business is doing is to calculate a profit and loss statement. Even though money may be coming in regularly through revenue from subscriptions and ancillary products, it may be possible that you are actually losing money because your expenses exceed your income.

Keeping accurate records will help make preparing a profit and loss statement much easier; all you have to do is plug in the numbers. There are two kinds of profit and loss statements you can keep: one that projects your estimated profits and losses, and another that keeps track on a weekly or monthly basis to help you see how well your newsletter is doing. You can also compare the two, and if your projections are either 20 percent higher or lower than your actual figures, based on slow and peak times, this method will enable you to adjust your projected profit and loss statements as you go along.

To figure out your profit and loss statement for your newsletter, you must first calculate the revenues you expect to generate each week, month and/or year. Say your newsletter costs $54 a year, and you project that you'll bring in 300 subscriptions in your first year. The total revenue is $16,200. You also sell ancillary products, and estimate that five percent of your subscribers—or 15 readers—will spend an average of $20 extra a year, which is $300.

The total gross revenue, based on these figures, then, is $16,500. At this point I'd play around with the numbers, adjusting them upward and downward to see how your revenues would change. In addition, you should think about the work that is necessary in order to generate 300 subscribers: I'll tell you now that it's a lot harder than it looks.

As you can see, publishing a newsletter won't be a huge money-maker for you in the beginning, but wait; you haven't even gotten to your expenses yet. Get out the list of operating costs you drew up in Chapter 6, and again, using either actual figures or estimates, add up all of your expenses for the year. You'll include postage, printing costs, phone bills, rent and utilities, business loans, everything.

And don't forget about depreciation. Ask your accountant for advice on this, but chances are that you'll be able to deduct the amount that is deemed to depreciate on your house, office equipment, and other big-ticket items this year. This is not strictly an expense, but will serve to help lower your profit, which will then lower your tax bill.

Don't forget about the interest you pay on any loans connected with the business. And remember that the type of business you run—sole proprietorship, partnership, or corporation—will also affect your profit and loss statement.

After deducting all of your expenses from your revenue, you'll be left with a pretax profit or loss. There's one more step, though. Now deduct all of the taxes you pay in connection with your business—except payroll taxes, which are figured into your payroll expenses—and you will come up with your actual net profit or loss, which probably seems a long way from your initial gross revenue figure.

Though you'll always have certain fixed expenses, there are a variety of ways you can adjust your profit and loss statement: cutting your expenses, discounting or raising your subscription rates (which I don't recommend), and increasing your marketing efforts are just a few. Over time, you will be able to see what attracts new subscribers and what keeps old subscribers renewing. You'll also see that publishing a newsletter is a constant experiment; your profit and loss statement is merely a constant reminder of how well your experiment is doing.

## Keeping Track of Your Money

Most newsletter publishers use a variety of methods to help them keep track of their money, both revenue and expenses.

The basic record will probably be your checkbook. There are a number of business checking accounts that come with built-in ledgers where you can record your expenses under different expense categories at the same time you write a check.

Separating these expenses in advance makes it easy at the end of the year to determine how much you've spent in each category, and if you need to cut back.

Some newsletter publishers prefer to keep their financial records on computer. Software now exists to enable you to keep track of your expenses, categorize them, add them up in a flash, and even write checks that are printed by your computer printer.

To keep track of your revenue, you should keep a record of each subscriber, the length of their subscription, and how much they paid, how they heard about you, and whether they've bought anything else from you. There are a number of specialized software programs that can help you keep track of your revenue and expenses, plus provide other features like word processing and database tracking.

Whatever method you choose, make sure that it's easy to use and that you check in with it at least once a week. Going longer than that will make keeping track of your money a chore and something you're likely to put off, which will make it more likely that you'll make mistakes.

Fortunately, some of the companies that you'll do business with are making it easier for their customers to keep track of their money. Credit and charge card companies now offer a breakdown of charges in different categories on their monthly statement. Some of the suppliers with which you maintain an account will also provide this service. And if they don't already do this, ask. They might start.

## Developing Your Credit

If you're in business for any length of time, you're going to need credit in one form or another. Most of the time, it will be from suppliers who deal with you on a regular basis and who don't deal in picking up cash or checks with each delivery they make. Not only is it too unwieldy and increases the possibility of loss, it's a big waste of time.

But most suppliers and other companies won't offer you credit unless you've done business with them before. It's the age-old Catch 22—how can you develop your credit if no one will give you any in the first place?

Fortunately, there are ways around this. Many companies will open a credit line for you based on your personal credit record. They'll usually start you out small, and then increase your credit line as your history with them grows. Needless to say, you'll help your credit line if you always pay promptly, even before the due date—and by acting promptly whenever they or you have questions about your account.

With other suppliers, you'll need to prove yourself in the beginning, and your personal credit, no matter how stellar, will have nothing to do with it. These companies will make you pay cash or by check before they deliver the goods, and only after a certain period of time will they begin to extend you credit, and only a little at a time at first.

Once you begin to establish a credit record for your publishing business, you'll undoubtedly be solicited by charge card companies that invite you to open a business account with a high credit limit and low monthly payments. Though having a business credit card account helps in many instances—such as renting a car or buying airline tickets in certain situations—try not to use them too much. When cards are almost universally accepted—even the IRS takes MasterCard and Visa now—because it's easier to slap down the plastic than to apply for a basic account with a supplier, you might be tempted to run up huge bills with their inherent high interest charges. This is a high price to pay for apparent convenience. Instead, use them sparingly, appreciate them for what they are—an extremely expensive way to borrow money—and be as judicious with their use and payment as you are with your other creditors. After all, they can help develop your credit rating, too.

And although banks are a lot pickier now about lending money to people with even unblemished credit ratings, you might apply for a line of credit at your bank, that is, if you don't have one already. Learning to rely on it only in emergency financial situations, then paying back the money immediately will help your business get through the tough times, and you will have them.

## Working with Suppliers

As I've already said, one part of working with suppliers is to build up credit, and a working relationship. There are other ways as well.

Getting the best price may be the most important thing to you. Other newsletter publishers might be attracted by a printer's twice-weekly pickup and dropoff schedule, while still others might favor a supplier because of the particular brands the company carries.

Most suppliers will bend over backwards to get your business, though you may find that you'll have to jump through a few hoops at first, for instance, to get a credit account set up in your initial dealings with the company.

There are many ways to find the suppliers who will work with you and who you'll feel most comfortable working with. You should know if one supplier doesn't give you the terms you'd like, there are others who will. Don't sign on with one right away—take the time to shop around for the best price, the quality you want, and the working relationship you feel comfortable with. Whether you prefer to deal by mail, have the items delivered to your door, or pick them up yourself, it's easy to find the best supplier for your newsletter business, from subscription premiums to paper for your laser printer.

## Borrowing Money

The issue of borrowing money in these credit-weary days is apt to be a sticky one among newsletter publishers who may have taken out a loan to finance their businesses. "I'm in enough debt already," you may say. "Why would I want to borrow any more?"

As you'll see in an upcoming section later in this chapter, sometimes your cash flow won't keep up with your expenses. Even if you and/or a partner holds down a steady job, trust me when I say there will be times when even that won't be enough. Operating a business and publishing a regular newsletter with all of the expenses that continue steadily from month to month will eat up huge amounts of cash, and during those times, it may be necessary to borrow money.

If you have a rich relative or a sizable trust fund, you can skip over this section. But if you're like most of us, you'll need to rely on a conventional financing source. And since you already know to anticipate these cycles, especially in a business that's usually known for its peaks and valleys throughout the year, you should take steps now to line up an available source of credit that you can draw upon immediately.

I know of many examples where newsletter publishers have drawn on their credit cards to initially finance their newsletters, and then have gone back to them when things got slow. At anywhere from a 12 percent to 21 percent annual rate of interest, this is definitely an expensive way to borrow money. Even if you fully intend to pay it back before interest has a chance to accumulate, there will be times when you are only able to make the minimum payment.

Some newsletter publishers form partnerships solely for this reason: to have a silent partner with deep pockets who's looking for a good rate of return on his or her money. But if you prefer to have a partner for other reasons—or to go it alone—and you don't want to have to rely on your credit cards, there is another option, and that is to open a line of credit at your bank.

If you don't want to go this route—or get turned down for it—there is the old-fashioned way, and that is to save for a rainy day. When business is booming and revenue is strong, set aside a certain percentage—some say 20 percent of every subscription that comes in—and sock it away in an interest-bearing savings account. Don't invest it in a place where you don't have instant access to your funds—even though the interest rate may be less, you'll probably pay more by paying a penalty for early withdrawal from an IRA, mutual fund, or other investment. A money market fund is best; the interest rates tends to be a little higher than a passbook savings account, and you have immediate access to your money.

## How to Raise Additional Capital

Because the revenue from a newsletter can be sporadic at times, many newsletter publishers turn to other sources of income. Most other businesses are concerned with raising additional capital to initially finance their business—even though their cash flow may be cyclical, the ups and downs are probably not as extreme as the cash flow in a newsletter publishing business. And if you need to raise additional capital to finance your newsletter, some people turn to parents or relatives, while many rely on the proceeds from the sale of their primary house and move in order to start their publication in an area where they can live mortgage free in order to plow all the revenue from the newsletter back into the business. For others with mortgages and no regular income, the best way to raise the additional capital needed to keep your newsletter afloat is to offer products and services connected with your business that you can sell to subscribers and non-subscribers alike. I provided some workable suggestions in Chapter 1; others include consulting and running seminars for people who aspire to be in your field or otherwise improve themselves in some way—remember, you're an expert now—publishing a collection of your most requested back issues, selling mugs,

T-shirts, and caps with the logo of your newsletter imprinted on it.

You have to be creative to stay in business these days, no matter what your venture is. The advantage of other services that you offer is that many of them will result in additional business for your newsletter, thus bringing your efforts full-circle.

## How to Give Credit to Customers

The primary way that most newsletter publishers extend credit to their customers is by accepting the several major types of credit cards that are popularly used today. MasterCard, Visa, American Express, and Discover are accepted by many newsletter publishers. The credit card companies will charge a fee to set you up with their service, and then you'll pay the credit card company a percentage of every transaction made by a customer, usually two to five percent. Your account is typically credited within one to three days after you entered the transactions into the system, and there are certain restrictions each company places on its members, depending on the amount your newsletter will gross each year, among other factors. It is relatively simple to apply for privileges that will allow you to accept credit cards from your patrons, although you may have to jump through a few hoops with financial statements, tax returns, checking account statements, and other proof that you run a trustworthy business and you won't go out of business six months down the road.

The reasons? It may seem unfair, but credit card companies like to grant merchant status to retail businesses with an actual storefront because in this business, the staff is handling actual credit cards, and customers see the total amount on the slip they are signing. Mail-order businesses are immediately suspect because they're not dealing with the physical card. Instead, you enter numbers into a small terminal and it's both easier to make a mistake and it's entirely possible to debit hundreds of thousands of dollars from account numbers you can punch in at random, wait until the money is deposited to your account, and then hit the road where you can live comfortably under an alias for the rest of your days. Don't laugh—this was the explanation that was given to me when I was turned down for merchant credit card status by one company.

Fortunately, the one place that I had been warned it would be almost impossible to receive credit card merchant status ended up being the one who accepted my newsletter publishing business with a personal recommendation: my bank. At the time I applied, my bank manager was familiar with the amount of money that was flowing in and out of my business account, which helped to establish the fact that my business was here to stay; plus, I had been banking with them for six years.

My advice is to keep looking and applying until you are accepted, because your revenues will instantly increase once you start to accept credit cards. If you decide against it, you may never know how profitable you may have become. Indeed, whether or not you accept credit cards may make the difference between whether or not your business succeeds or not. Unfortunate, but true. Before I started taking credit cards, one man sent me his credit card number with instructions to start his subscription. I wrote back and told him we weren't set up to accept plastic yet, and to send a check. I never heard from him again.

However, some newsletter publishers decide not to accept charge cards from their subscribers. Either their volume is too low to justify paying the commissions, or else the credit company places too many restrictions on them. Some have also said that the companies tend to have a patronizing attitude toward smaller companies—such as newsletter publishers—because they simply don't provide the commission revenue that larger businesses do.

Others just figure that if subscribers want to receive their newsletter, they'll subscribe whether they pay for it with a credit card or a check. But as I've already said, newsletters are often an impulse buy, and credit cards capitalize on this perfectly.

Occasionally, a potential subscriber will ask if you can bill him or her. Personally, my subscription list is not set up to keep track of who's been invoiced and who hasn't, and who paid and who hasn't. In my opinion, it only adds to the paperwork, which you don't need any more of. I've also discovered that most people use it as a way to get a free sample issue. As a result, most never subscribe. I've tested this theory, however, by sending a bill when requested, *without* an issue enclosed. In all cases, I've never heard from them again.

Any way you decide to extend credit to customers, it's important that you do offer it in some form. We have a love-hate relationship with it as a society. But since we do rely on it, you should arrange for it before you start publishing your newsletter, if at all possible.

## Improving Cash Flow

Even though publishing your newsletter will be a business where the cash flow will be highly erratic at times, you can, to some extent, predict when your cash flow will slow down and when it will be high. This will help you to see which months you should stockpile some of your excess cash in order to provide you with cash flow and income in the down times.

Cash flow is defined as the pattern of movement of cash in and out of a business: revenue and expenses. If you apply for a loan with a bank or other financial company after your business is up and running, you'll have to provide an analysis of your cash flow; if you're just starting out, you may be required to provide the loan officer with a projected cash flow statement.

Cash flow includes all actual monies coming in and going out of the business, and includes cash, checks, and income from credit cards. Depreciation of your computer and other office equipment does not factor into your cash flow analysis.

The first step to improving your cash flow is to increase your business year-round. But the effects from this aren't always that immediate, and there are thing you can do to even out your cash flow a little more.

Tying in with your own cash flow projections, you might want to conduct special promotions designed to pull in more subscriptions during those times of the year when your cash flow needs boosting the most. For instance, you should plan to mail subscription offers to your expired subscribers in your slow months. Or you can send out direct mail packages offering your ancillary items to past and present subscribers as well as those who have never subscribed.

Another way to even out your expenses and therefore improve your cash flow is to ask your utility companies to average out your payments so that you basically pay the same amount each month year-round. And as I suggested earlier, if you stash away 20 percent of your gross revenue during the busy times, you'll have money to draw on during the slow months.

## Action Guidelines

✔ Calculate what your gross revenue would be with a variety of different subscription figures over the course of a year.

✔ Subtract your projected expenses from the totals for your estimated gross revenues to determine your profit or loss for the year.

✔ Work with your suppliers to eventually develop a credit history that's based on your newsletter and not your own personal credit rating.

✔ Select your financial source to help you through the slow seasons, whether it's a business partner or money that you've saved from peak times.

✔ Arrange with credit card companies so you can accept charge cards from your subscribers.

## Newsletter Publisher Profile

### Dana Cassell
### *Freelance Writer's Report*

Dana Cassell knew she was onto something when she was working full-time as a freelance writer in Florida and attended her first writing seminar, to discover that she knew more about the business than the person giving the seminar. In fact, another person at the seminar told Cassell that she should be the one up there teaching instead. "I filed that one away," she says.

In the course of her freelance writing, she frequently talked with a lot of editors who told her that they needed other people to write stories for them besides Dana. That stuck in her mind as well. "I envisioned an organization of writers that editors could regularly contact for work, and also thought about doing workshops to help them get more work," she said. She looked in the directory *Writers Market* and found that it listed 65 magazines in Florida. But she did a little research and discovered that there were actually 300 magazines that were based in the state.

And so she started the Florida Freelance Writer's Association, where members would receive an annual directory of Florida markets, a four-page monthly newsletter, and a Writer Databank Referral Service to make it easy for editors to contact members in the group. Once editors began to learn they could find Florida writers through the association, they began to ask for writers in other states. This didn't turn out to be a problem, since Cassell says that FFWA has always had members who lived in other states simply because her organization was doing things that no other writer's group was doing. "But I didn't want to start a separate organization, database and newsletter for every state, so I increased the newsletter to eight pages, and for the Florida members—who paid more—I inserted a special Florida section of four pages," says Cassell. She then began to market just the newsletter to a national audience and put national information in the publication as well as expanding the databank.

Then, in February of 1993, she decided to move north to New Hampshire. A number of factors influenced her decision, besides the fact that she was tired of the crowds and crime in Florida. She was running her business over the telephone, fax, and mail, anyway, so it wasn't a big decision to make the move. "Some people say they wish we were still down there even though they only talk to us by phone," says Dana. "I have an 800 line, and I think some people think we're still down there."

When her business was still in Florida, Dana did a lot of the promotion for it by doing seminars. She would conduct monthly seminars all over the state. The workshops would range from one-day to half-day and evening seminars. Sometimes she conducted them herself, while for others she'd invite other writers to run them.

"Seminars turned out to be a good marketing tool, since you can hold a seminar and set the price so that people get a newsletter subscription along with their workshop," says Cassell. "But doing all of the business and planning for the seminars was taking all of my time so that I had no time left to write, which wasn't my original intention."

In addition to the seminars, she also ran an annual conference, targeted towards established writers, that she held each year for twelve years. In fact, Cassell held a conference in Florida the first year she was living in New Hampshire, and decided to discontinue it after that. "The conference business in Florida is different than it used to be, more expensive and more competitive, so once I moved up north I decided not to risk it," she says. During the years she was running the conference, she would plan for several hundred people to show up, along with numerous speakers, and a $50,000 budget to boot.

Since she moved out of Florida, Cassell says that overall the number of her Florida subscribers has gone down, but she attributes that to the fact that she's no longer running the seminars. "I would get people who would join the Association only because they got a free seminar," she said. "In the end, I found I was continually treading water to replace those people with more by giving more free seminars. After awhile, I decided that I would rather let my total circulation reach a number of really serious people who would be with me no matter what."

*Freelance Writers Report* is a monthly newsletter. Cassell charges $39 a year and sends it out bulk rate. She also has published a few small books and booklets about writing and has 42 different Special Reports. Though she sells the Special Reports, she says that their greatest value comes from using them as premiums to attract new subscribers and get old ones to renew.

The advice she has for new newsletter publishers is similar to what other publishers offer: "The first thing you have to do is find a list you can rent, because if you can't rent a list, then that means there's no audience," she says. "The only way I can see a newsletter being successful is if you use a tightly targeted list. If you want to get enough money to bankroll your first few issues, you should put on a free seminar so that you have lots of people writing and calling for information, and build a list from those names. Then put together a good direct mail package and send it out."

# THE GROWTH OF
# YOUR BUSINESS

G rowing a business today can be a challenge. Though everything you will do as a newsletter publisher will in some way influence how your business grows, most of the time your thoughts will not be on growth, but on putting out all of the little fires that will pop up each day. If you have any time or energy left at the end of the day to think about growth, it may be along the lines of how to slow it down so that you'll have at least 15 minutes each day to call your own.

Seriously, growth—or the lack of it—is an issue that every newsletter publisher has to face at one time or another. This last chapter will show you how to deal with the variety of ways that growth will manifest itself in the business of publishing your newsletter. And if you've gotten this far in your determination to publish your own newsletter, handling growth will probably turn out to be the least of your troubles.

## The Problems of Business Growth

Many newsletter publishers feel that of all the business problems to have, those that involve issues of growth are among the easiest to handle.

It's not always so. Though growth as a rule means increased revenue and business, it also means more work and expenses, as well as more headaches to deal with.

Some newsletters will grow at a slow steady rate of 8 percent to 10 percent a year. Others will explode after a glowing article—complete with subscription price and contact information—in a large-circulation magazine or newspaper appears. Which is better? While some prefer slow growth as a way to allow them to learn about the business and grow into it, others say that rapid and/or sudden growth provides them with a real education of what publishing a newsletter is all about, and provides a needed boost to the business when the owner might have otherwise been hesitant about forging ahead. This kick in the pants is sometimes exactly what a newsletter publisher needs.

Growth *can* be managed and controlled to some extent. How you do it and whether you do, however, is up to you.

Some of the choice is manifested in the ability to limit the number of subscribers through subscription price and limited direct mail over the course of a year. Indeed, there are a handful of newsletters that pride themselves on their exclusivity and do indeed limit the number of subscribers, but you're probably not in this category.

One issue you'll face with a growing newsletter is whether or not to hire employees—or if you already have help, whether you should increase their hours to full-time or hire more workers.

Your newsletter is your baby, and if you're used to doing it all yourself you may find it hard to delegate some of the responsibility to someone else, even if it means more free time for you. Most newsletter publishers have difficulty letting go at first, but with time and as you begin to see the high level of the ability of the people you do hire, you will trust in them more, which will leave you with time to turn to other problems in the business that need to be addressed.

Another by-product of growth is what to do with the extra money. Some newsletter publishers use it to pay off some of their personal debts, but the IRS will count these monies as personal income. It's best to do this over time, though some people feel that the savings you'll make in not paying debt interest will more than offset the increased tax you'll have to pay.

Some newsletter publishers use the extra money to pay off their home mortgages. Though it may feel good to own your own house free and clear, the interest you'll be able to deduct from your mortgage payment each month for your home business office can come in handy in keeping your taxes down, especially since your business will likely show a larger profit with increased income.

One method that many newsletter publishers use to invest the money and keep their profits and therefore their taxes down at the same time is to upgrade office equipment and purchase a new phone system or the latest desktop system each year. This will not only cut your taxes, but you'll be able to streamline your operation and also handle more volume, which will increase your revenue—*and* your profits—so that next year you'll have to do the same thing all over again. Granted, though, it's a nice problem to have. Of course, as I explained in Chapter 6, you will have to show a profit three out of five years if you're operating as a sole proprietorship or partnership, but if you've been growing steadily, this will not be a problem.

## Managing Employees for Greatest Efficiency

The art of management once prescribed that a boss or manager should rule with an iron grip in one hand and a whip in the other. Just like any strict disciplinarian parent, both employer and employees knew who was in charge. Employees went along with this facade, but more often than not, managed to get away with things whenever they could, did only what was expected of them, and never anything more.

The opposite philosophy was that of the sensitive manager. He or she soft-pedaled harsh news, coddled his employees, and always was ready to heap lavish praise at the tiniest accomplishment. Again, employees went along with it, but felt they were never fully trusted or appreciated for their own talents and efforts. As before, quality and morale suffered.

The ideal management style for a small newsletter publishing business is to let employees feel as though they are responsible for the business's success or failure; that is, they treat it as though it were their own, which comes with certain responsibilities.

This style is perfect for newsletter publishers who need to delegate, and also because newsletter staffers will work very closely with you and therefore tend to quickly develop a personal relationship with the boss. This type of management may run counter to what many people think being a boss ought to be, but in the end, you'll find that your employees will be happier, more productive, and will also stay with you longer if you learn to manage them in this way.

It's not easy to do this, however. People who feel they have to control their employees in order to get them to work may run into problems with executing this altered style of management. However, once you see that your employees will treat your business almost as well as you do, it won't take long for you to become a proponent of this management style and actually begin to adopt it in other areas of your life.

Here's how to do it. Say you need to hire an employee to work 20 hours a week at your newsletter, helping out wherever you happen to need it. First, determine the tasks he or she is best at, and which of those he or she would feel comfortable being left alone to execute.

Train by going through the various tasks this employee will need to become familiar with, from answering the phone to taking phone orders to printing out a press release on the computer. Have him or her watch you do it a few times, and then let your new employee do it alone. Assure your employee that he or she can approach you with any questions, no matter how trivial they may seem. Encourage open communication at all times. Your end of the deal is to remain open to queries and always respond in a patient manner.

Then, once it appears he or she has one task down pat, give him or her another one. For instance, if he or she is comfortable with taking phone orders, you might let him or her take the next logical step, entering the information into the computer, sending out welcome letters to new subscribers with their first issue with perhaps a handwritten note.

If your employee makes any mistakes, call them to his or her attention immediately, and then patiently and without judgment, explain the way to do it that's best for the newsletter and *why*. Make sure that it's not just because the new employee is doing the tasks a bit differently from how you would do it. In fact, for maximum efficiency, try not to get too caught up with how things get done, rather, that they *do* get done. If you insist that your employees follow certain steps in order to reach the final solution, you'll find that you'll be trying to squeeze a lot of round pegs into square holes. The outcome may turn out the same, but the morale may not, and your efficiency will, as a result, probably drop.

Then, as your employees' responsibilities grow, increase their pay based on performance and give regular bonuses and days off with pay. The idea is for employees to feel personally responsible for the subscribers' satisfaction so that your time is freed up to work on other projects without worrying about the business.

The secret to successfully managing employees is to show them what to do, trust that they'll do it, and then leave them alone. Though many employees will be taken aback by this unique approach, and some will find it to be too alien for their tastes, the great majority will meet the challenge and help to build your business while cultivating a personal relationship with you.

What works best is to show your employee what the final result should look like, and then go off and do your own thing. As long as the basic quality of the job isn't compromised, it helps to learn to look the other way. Some newsletter publishers are perfectionists, however, and they think that no one but themselves knows how to do things the right way. Unfortunately, this kind of manager will find it hard to keep employees, and may be burned out by the end of their first year in the business.

Though you're still calling the shots, compromise and acceptance is the name of the game when it comes to managing employees and maintaining the steady growth of your newsletter.

## Secrets of Success

In my opinion, along with many other newsletter publishers nationwide, the number one key to success in the industry is through marketing. In this instance, I use the term quite loosely: not only does marketing encompass all of the traditional channels, like advertising and publicity, but it also includes your own personal public relations campaign, or how you interact with your public, that is, your subscribers.

During every minute that a subscriber is exposed to your business—either on the phone or through the mail and with each and every issue of your newsletter—you should be marketing your business in a positive light. I'm not talking about the hard sell; after all, they're already subscribers. The secret of success is to get them to renew their subscriptions, and to tell their friends about the value of subscribing to your newsletter. This means being constantly aware of whether or not the newsletter is meeting their needs, and if there's anything more you can do to improve on what you're already doing. However, you should expect that some subscribers won't welcome this degree of personal interaction with you; in these cases, you'll have to let your newsletter do your marketing for you.

But remember, your marketing job never ends, and that goes for both kinds: through the media and every issue of your newsletter. If you cease to market, you will soon fade from your subscribers' memory because it's obvious you didn't care enough about their satisfaction. After all, with thousands of messages bombarding them each day, you need to stand out to succeed. But that doesn't mean a constant hard sell, either.

Oh, and your happiness and satisfaction are also keys to success in the newsletter publishing business.

## Two Typical Problems and Solutions

Though each newsletter business will face its own unique set of problems, there are some problems that most newsletter publishers will face at one time or another. Here are two of the most common, along with some solutions.

1. *I know I should put money away to help pay the bills when business slows down, but there are always so many other bills that demand my attention that I never seem to get around to it. Also, I'm working so hard putting out each issue that I feel I deserve a reward. Help!*

A: Consider putting money aside for your rainy days the same way as you pay your bills. Decide in advance the percentage of your gross deposits that you're going to put into savings, and then do it automatically when you go to the bank.

The amount of 10 or 20 percent may not seem like a lot, but it does add up. And keep in mind that the reasons why a number of newsletters fail is because they don't have enough cash to make it through the downtimes. The owner may decide to take a job in the interim, which will definitely interfere with his or her ability to keep attracting new subscribers, that is, if he or she intended to publish the newsletter as a full-time business when it was begun. So keep stashing it away.

As for rewards, the best kind of treat any newsletter publisher can give is some spare time, which doesn't cost anything. So whether you go out for an afternoon, or take yourself to the movies, consider this to be the best reward you could give yourself. But you probably already know this.

2. *Publishing a newsletter keeps me extremely busy running around each day, but by the end of the day I look back and I don't seem to have accomplished much. The problem is that the phone rings whenever I'm in the middle of something, or I'm interrupted by something else. What can I do?*

A: Learn to make lists, delegate, and take advantage of the quiet times that do occur in the course of each day. Some chronic list-makers, however, regularly put more on their list than they could ever hope to accomplish in a week, let alone a day. If you fall into this category, start by chopping your list in half, or even by three-fourths. That way, if you check off everything on your list and there are still a few hours in the day, you can always add a few more.

You'll find that most work at a newsletter gets done in short spurts in between a variety of interruptions, though most owners would prefer to have quiet, uninterrupted periods of time in which to work Your task is to make an effort to schedule more uninterrupted periods during the day in order to allow you to concentrate on your work.

The best way to do this is to let someone else play the front person for you. Have somebody answer the phone for a few afternoons each week—or let the answering machine take the calls. To make sure that you're not interrupted, leave the office and go someplace where you can get some work done. Retreat to a far corner of the house, seek refuge at a friend's house, or even go to the library.

If this is impossible, or if you find you need even more time, you might want to take advantage of the time of the day when there will be the least amount of demands on your time. If you're not ready to crash, late night can be a marvelous quiet time when you can accomplish office or other work.

The trick is to find what works best for you and then stick to it, because it will always be extremely easy to let the day slide into night working 12 or more hours a day, but with the feeling that you got absolutely nothing done.

## Reality Check

Every newsletter publisher has experienced a time when they've been so busy, or so involved with their business, that they have learned to tune out the world as a whole and not venture beyond the office except to go grocery shopping. Some even get someone else to perform these outside tasks for them.

When you start your newsletter business, you'll probably be operating your business from your home. If you're used to commuting to an office every day, you should be prepared for a shock, because you'll have to motivate yourself, and there will be no one else around to do it. In addition, the constant interruptions and lack of personal time can quickly begin to skew your perspective on life and the world. Even if you have regular contact with lots of people over the phone, if you don't venture out at least a few times a week, it's entirely possible that your attitude will begin to change.

That's why it's imperative to get away from the business for a full afternoon or evening at least once a week. Or take one day a week off. Do something that has nothing to do with the business. Do something for yourself for an extended period of time, or else, you'll need to refer to the next section a little sooner than necessary.

## When to Quit

Burnout and overfamiliarization with their subject are the major reasons why newsletter publishers decide to sell or close down their businesses. It's so very easy to become caught up in running your business—after all, you are actually giving a performance of sorts to your subscribers, and all that attention and praise can be very gratifying to the ego—so that you may reach the point where you have no desire to do anything else. This is precisely why many newsletter publishers keep doing more and more of it, and why a few choose not to hire employees even if they need the extra help desperately.

Another reason why newsletter publishers decide to get out of the business is closely tied in with reason number one: publishing a successful newsletter—or an unsuccessful one, for that matter—is a lot more difficult than it appears on the surface. They underestimate the amount of work and overestimate the money that the newsletter will generate—especially the money they think will be available for their own personal use.

Because of these skewed expectations, people tend to quit the business long before the time they plan to otherwise leave. Five years is frequently cited as the typical amount of time a

189 • The Growth of Your Business

newsletter publisher will be in business before he or she gets the feeling it's time to move on to something else.

You'll know it's time to quit when:

- you no longer become excited about a new development in your topic;
- you can't remember the last time you took a vacation;
- you worked through the holidays;
- you can't remember the last time you woke up feeling refreshed;
- you're so burned out you've lost your enthusiasm for most things.

Of course, newsletter publishers who still love what they're doing may feel one or all of these symptoms at one time or another. But the secret to knowing when to quit is when you feel like moving on and believe the disadvantages of publishing a newsletter outweigh the advantages.

You may decide to opt out of the business, and in fact, may sell your business to someone who's new to the field. ("Remember when we were that enthusiastic?" you may say.) But, as was my case, many newsletter publishers who leave the business jump right back in a few years later.

So take heed—once you start, you may not be able to stop. After all, publishing a newsletter will get in your blood.

**Action Guidelines**

✔ Be prepared not to enjoy every aspect of growth that your newsletter will experience.

✔ Learn to manage employees with a hands-off attitude.

✔ Keep in mind that marketing your newsletter is a nonstop venture.

✔ Keep your perspective on your life by taking regular breaks from the business.

## Newsletter Publisher Profile

### Barbara Radcliffe Rogers
### *Folk Arts Quarterly*

When Barbara Rogers started publishing her 12- to 16-page newsletter on old crafts techniques that were lost in time or perhaps not well known to people who were interested in crafts, it was both a labor of love as well as a promotional device. At the time, she was growing and drying herbs and other produce on her Heritage Farm in Richmond, New Hampshire. She was looking for a vehicle in order to advertise her herb craft and folk art kits, clothespin and corn husk crafts kits, as well as a new way to build up new markets for the kits. Rogers could test kits in the newsletter, to see if people would be interested in them.

She started publishing her newsletter in a conservative fashion. "Before I started working on my first issue, I bought an ad in a crafts magazine that reached the crowd I was interested in. I also sent notices to all the major crafts magazines, most of which printed my information since I was writing articles for them at the time," she said. She had planned in advance what her mailing and printing costs would be to send out each issue, but she didn't proceed with publishing the newsletter until she had received a certain number of subscribers. In fact, she held onto the checks for about a month until she knew it was a go.

Rogers did all the writing for the newsletter herself. She didn't have a computer, so she used an electronic memory typewriter to set the columns and then laid them out by hand. She also drew all of the illustrations and line drawings that appeared in the newsletter. "My logo looked very much like the labels on my kits, which added to the newsletter's marketing value," she added.

Rogers published *Folk Arts Quarterly* for five years before discontinuing the newsletter. Her reasons? "I had enough subscribers, but I thought my renewal wasn't tremendous, only about 50 percent. Toward the end, I got down to a nitty gritty core subscriber list who frequently corresponded with me and always renewed their subscriptions, but the newsletter wasn't growing, and I had stopped doing solicitations. It became very time consuming, and more importantly, the people who were subscribing were not buying my kits."

"Looking back, if I had it to do over again, I would have done it on a computer, but maybe not," she says. "I also would have put more effort into trying to identify the market a little more closely and to identify catalog suppliers that supplied that market. I also would have worked to accept some advertising. I didn't take ads because I didn't think that my circulation warranted it. I always thought that if the newsletter didn't work out I could stop publishing it quickly. Once you've taken someone's ad money, it becomes more difficult to stop publishing."

Though today Rogers concentrates on writing travel articles and books, she says that she much preferred writing for her own newsletter. "After all, I had my own format," she says. "Other magazines had their own format and they wanted their instructions presented in a certain way. Also, I had the freedom to work with subject matter the magazines either weren't interested in or weren't promoting in their advertising mission.

"Publishing a newsletter gave me total freedom. If you're a writer, the best thing in the world is to have your own column and get to know your readers. With the newsletter, I was doing that on a regular basis with a whole bunch of articles."

*Appendix*

**A**

# SAMPLE BUSINESS PLAN

*Antiques & Collectibles Business*

Williams Hill Publishing
Grafton, New Hampshire 03240

A Business Plan for a Newsletter
by Lisa Angowski Rogak
Williams Hill Publishing

## STATEMENT OF PURPOSE

This business plan will serve as an operational guide and general policy manual for *Antiques & Collectibles Business.*

Williams Hill Publishing is looking to publish a newsletter for men and women who work in the antiques and collectibles business full- or part-time. This business plan will serve as a blueprint to launch the newsletter, and then to steer it successfully.

The launch of the newsletter *Antiques & Collectibles Business* will be self-financed.

# TABLE OF CONTENTS

# SECTION ONE: THE BUSINESS

## A. Description of Business

*Antiques & Collectibles Business* will be a newsletter that will help men and women who sell antiques and collectibles to run their businesses more effectively. *Antiques & Collectibles Business* will be published eight times a year, and a one-year subscription will cost $35.

In addition to subscribing to the newsletter, Williams Hill Publishing will produce a number of ancillary products to sell through the newsletter, including back issues, Special Reports, and books, including the publisher's book *The Upstart Guide to Owning & Managing an Antiques Business*.

*Antiques & Collectibles Business* will contain information about financing, staffing, marketing, expansion, and other relevant topics, along with profiles of successful antiques entrepreneurs in every issue. It will pertain to both novice antiques entrepreneurs and those in the intermediate stages of running their businesses.

## B. Description of the Market

Most people who enter the antiques business get into it by accident. Collectors at heart, perhaps one day they saw a piece they just couldn't live without, but to finance the purchase, they had to part with some of their present hoard. Maybe they made a few phone calls and it was sold, the new piece in their possession shortly after.

"That was easy," they think, and start to consider doing the show circuit or renting a booth in a mall in order to finance even larger acquisitions—either intending to make a living at it or to just pull in some money on the side.

The main problem these people run into is that they may have a full-fledged business, but they're still running it like a hobby.

That's where *Antiques & Collectibles Business* comes in. The newsletter will show these people how to take their businesses seriously so that their businesses grow.

Williams Hill Publishing will pursue subscribers in several different areas:

- Publicity in antiques newspapers and other consumer magazines and newspapers;
- Antiques show appearances with booth rentals and seminars and workshops;
- Co-op marketing with other antiques publications;
- Direct marketing to selected rented lists and to buyers of the publisher's book.

## C. Description of the Competition

Though there are hundreds of specialized publications that cover antiques, none focus specifically on how to run an antiques business. Occasionally, a few of these papers will run a story on taxes or marketing, but for the most part, these publications concentrate on reviewing antiques shows and auctions, and on spotlighting a particular period of antique.

*Antiques & Collectibles Business* will be the first of its kind.

## D. Description of Management

Lisa Angowski Rogak has served as publisher and editor of two of Williams Hill Publishing's other newsletters: *Sticks* and *Travel Marketing Bulletin*. She launched both publications, is actively promoting them and building each newsletter to their current subscriber levels of 1000 and 300 subscribers, respectively.

She has conducted marketing and publicity campaigns for other publishers, and has hired an employee to deal with the day-to-day operations of the newsletters, leaving her free to concentrate on marketing and promotion.

Williams Hill Publishing plans to join several regional antiques associations as an associate member in order to keep tabs on the industry and network with local antiques entrepreneurs.

## E. Description of Personnel

Williams Hill Publishing has hired one part-time employee to assume responsibility for the editing of *Antiques & Collectibles Business,* under the guidance of the publisher. The employee will be paid $10 an hour to start, working two days a week, with no benefits. Additional weekend days will be made available for the editor during the show season in order to meet antiques dealers and pass out samples of the newsletter.

We don't anticipate the need for additional employees at this time.

## F. Expected Use of Initial Investment

Williams Hill Publishing intends to invest $2000 to launch *Antiques & Collectibles Business,* since all necessary office equipment is already owned by the business.

| | |
|---|---:|
| 1,000 copies of first issue printed | $250 |
| Initial press mailing of 400 copies, including printing, postage, and follow-up calls | $600 |
| 10 days editorial work to write, edit, and design first issue and press materials | $800 |
| Miscellaneous expenses | $350 |
| | $2,000 |

Williams Hill Publishing projects that it will take three to four months until regular revenue is being generated from the marketing efforts for *Antiques & Collectibles Business.* Early subscription fees that are received will finance the cost of producing subsequent issues until the newsletter is self-sustaining, sometime during the first six months. In addition, sales of *The Upstart Guide to Owning & Managing an Antiques Business* will also help to pay for publishing the newsletter during this period.

## G. Summary

Williams Hill Publishing projects that *Antiques & Collectibles Business* will be a thriving newsletter in two years, with 2,000 or more loyal subscribers. As more people look to strike out in their own business, the number of people in the antiques business will grow. Most of them will need some kind of guidance, and they'll find it in the pages of *Antiques & Collectibles Business.*

Though the newsletter is aimed towards beginning and intermediate antiques dealers—since there are simply more of them—we'd guess that even established antiques entrepreneurs would subscribe, if only to get some idea of what others are doing since *Antiques & Collectibles Business* will regularly feature profiles of successful antiques entrepreneurs.

# SECTION TWO: FINANCIAL DATA
## A. Cash Flow Statement

| | Jan. | Feb. | Mar. | Ap. | May | June | July | Aug. | Sept. | Oct. | Nov. | Dec. |
|---|---|---|---|---|---|---|---|---|---|---|---|---|
| Mortgage/Rent | $100 | 100 | 100 | 100 | 100 | 100 | 100 | 100 | 100 | 100 | 100 | 100 |
| Taxes | | | | | | | | | | | | |
| Insurance | | | | | | | | | | | | |
| Utilities | | | | | | | | | | | | |
| Heat | | | | | | | | | | | | |
| Office Expenses | | | | | | | | | | | | |
| Telephone | $100 | 200 | 100 | 100 | 100 | 100 | 100 | 100 | 100 | 100 | 100 | 100 |
| Fax line | $35 | 35 | 35 | 35 | 35 | 35 | 35 | 35 | 35 | 35 | 35 | 35 |
| Postage | $300 | 150 | 100 | 100 | 200 | 300 | 200 | 250 | 200 | 200 | 200 | 300 |
| Stationery & supplies | $350 | 175 | 100 | 100 | 125 | 100 | 100 | 100 | 275 | 100 | 125 | 100 |
| Printing | $400 | 50 | 100 | 200 | 200 | 200 | 200 | 250 | 500 | 200 | 200 | 200 |
| Advertising | | | | | | | | | | | | |
| **mailing list rentals | $400 | | | | 400 | | | | | 400 | | |
| **mailing house service | $200 | | | | 200 | | | | | 200 | | |
| Accountant fees | $350 | | | 150 | | | | | 250 | | | |
| Attorney fees | $500 | | | | | | | | | | | |
| Independent contractors | | $200 | | 200 | | 200 | | 200 | | 200 | | |
| Computer equipment | $2,000 | | | | | 400 | | | | | | |
| Software | $225 | | | | | 150 | | | | | | |

# SAMPLE MARKETING PLAN

I consider drawing up a marketing plan to be barely secondary to writing your business plan. Your business plan will serve as your anchor; a marketing plan will be your rudder. Again, it's important to take the time now to discover all your marketing options, and then choose the ones that will work the best for you.

Refer to the following plan when planning the marketing strategies for your business.

# Marketing Plan
## for
## *Antiques & Collectibles Business*

Williams Hill Publishing projects that approximately 15 percent of annual revenues will be spent on marketing. We project that 750 subscriptions will be sold in the first year of publication, generating $26,250 in revenue. Additional services and ancillary products will generate another $3,750 in revenue for an estimated $30,000 in revenue in the newsletter's first year of publication. Therefore, the publisher plans to spend approximately $4,500 in marketing costs in the first year alone.

The four major methods of marketing are detailed in the business plan. What follows is a month-by-month marketing plan:

*First Month:* Mail press kit and first issue of *AC&B* to 400 media names. One week later, make follow-up calls.

Approximate cost, including printing, postage, phone calls, and labor: $600.

*Second Month:* Send direct mail piece about *AC&B* to past mail-order purchasers of *The Upstart Guide to Owning & Managing an Antiques Business*. Prepare 3,000 pieces. This mailing will be small—only 500 names—but the direct mail package will be complete and ready to send out over the upcoming year whenever a potential subscriber calls or writes for more information.

Approximate cost:  Printing: $700
                   Postage: $150

Also, place 40 targeted editors on the subscription list at no cost to them.

Approximate cost: $20 an issue

***Third Month:*** Prepare a sheet of ancillary products and insert into third issue of *AC&B.*

Approximate cost: $50

***Fourth Month:*** The show season starts to get into full swing. Marketing now through September primarily consists of sending the editor of *AC&B* out one day each weekend to antiques shows and shops to distribute sample copies of *AC&B* and to talk it up.

Approximate cost: $75 a day, $300 a month

***Fifth Month:*** Editor appearances.

Approximate cost: $75 a day, $300 a month

***Sixth Month:*** Editor appearances.

Approximate cost: $75 a day, $300 a month

***Seventh Month:*** Editor appearances.

Approximate cost: $75 a day, $300 a month

***Eighth Month:*** Second press mailing to original media list of 400 names plus 100 new names we've targeted.

Approximate cost: $600

***Ninth Month:*** Send out mailing promoting *The Antiques Businessowner's Kit,* including a one-year subscription to *AC&B,* a copy of *The Upstart Guide to Owning & Managing an Antiques Business,* and two Special Reports for one package deal to give as a Christmas present.

Approximate cost: $500

***Tenth Month:*** Make follow-up calls for the Kit.

Approximate cost: $100

***Eleventh Month:*** Arrange with a regional antiques newspaper to insert a flyer for *AC&B.*

Approximate cost: $300

***Twelfth Month:*** Arrange with another regional antiques newspaper to insert a flyer for *AC&B.*

Approximate cost: $300

**Total annual marketing expenses: $4,520**

# INDEX

205-209; writing, 82; writing a, 70, 75

*Marketing with Newsletters,* Floyd, 119

Market Planning Assessment, 78-80

MasterCard, 144, 167

*Mayo Clinic Health Letter, The* 13

Media interviews, 157

Media kit. *See* Press kit

*Medical Abstracts,* 13

Microsoft: Publisher, 36; Works, 36

Money-back guarantee, 137

Money markets, 170

*Montana Magazine,* 130

Morrison, Dane, 84

*Ms.,* 22

Mutual funds, 170

**N**

Naming your newsletter, 90-93, 100

National associations, 60-61

National Writers Union, 150

Networking, 51, 62

Newsletter directories, 57-58, 88

Newsletter Association, The, 51

Newsletter Clearinghouse, The, 51

Newsletter Factory, The, 53

*Newsletter News & Resources,* 119

Newsletter objectives, 71-72

Newsletter publisher profiles, 21-25, 45-46, 63-65, 83-85, 101-103, 118-120, 159-161, 176-178, 191-192

Newsletter publishing: from home, 4

Newsletter publishing opportunities, 1

Newsletter resources, 47-61

Newsletters: advertising in, 145-146; association, 3, 13; business-oriented, 12, 139, 146; consumer, 13, 139; description, 2-4; frequency, 146-147; history of, 9; length, 2; pricing, 136-141; sample issues, 133-134, 138; special interest, 13; start-up, 16

Newspapers, 62

*New York Magazine,* 24

*New York Times,* 30

**O**

Office equipment, 181

Office supplies, 114-115

Open Horizons, 63

Operating costs, 105-109, 111, 164

Operations, daily, 5-9, 105, 112, 163

Opinion, 4, 10, 19

**P**

Padgett-Thompson, 52

PageMaker, 34, 118

Partnership, 94-96, 100, 115

Payroll expenses, 165

Payroll taxes, 113, 115-116, 165

Permits, 98, 100

Personal liability, 95

Phone orders. *See* Subscriptions, by phone

Phone systems, 16, 37-38, 40, 181

Phone with built-in answering machine, 36

Postage, 107

PR consultant, 128

Press clips, 133, 135

Press kit, 130, 132; creating a, 133-135

Printers, 36

Printing services, 57-58, 107, 113-114

Profit, 17, 116, 163-164, 175, 181

Profit and loss statement, 163-165

Promotion, 76, 106-107

Promotional material, 155-156

Publicity, 78, 129, 131, 156, 184; in other publications, 131-132; on radio, 131; on television, 131

Public speaking, 132

**Q**

Quark, 34, 36

**R**

Readership survey, 88

Records: financial, 98, 109-110, 164; of subscribers, 124

Referrals, 126

Registering business name, 91

Regulations, business, 93